Eyewitness Accounts of the American Revolution

Songs and Ballads
of the
American Revolution
Frank Moore

The New York Times & Arno Press

Songs and Ballads.

Songs and BALLADS of the

American Revolution.

Songs and Ballads

OF THE

AMERICAN REVOLUTION.

WITH NOTES AND ILLUSTRATIONS

BY

FRANK MOORE.

"More solid things do not shew the complexion of the Times so well, as *Ballads* and *Libels*." SELDEN.

NEW YORK:

D. APPLETON & COMPANY, 346 & 348 BROADWAY.

LONDON: 16 LITTLE BRITAIN.

MDCCCLVI.

PREFACE.

THIS volume presents a selection from the numerous productions in verse, which appeared during the war of the American Revolution. Many of them are taken from the newspapers and periodical issues of the time ; others from original ballad-sheets and broadsides ; while some have been received from the recollections of a few surviving soldiers, who heard and sang them amid the trials of the camp and field.

Nearly every company had its " smart one " or

poet, who beguiled the weariness of the march or the encampment by his minstrelsy, grave or gay ; and the imperfect fragments which survive to us, provoke our regret that so few of them have been preserved.

All that we can claim for the writers of these songs, is a manifest spirit of devotion to the cause, and defiance to its enemies. The poesy of their productions is meagre. They did not write for fame ; but, in the language of one of the most honest and homely of them, " from a great desire to state the truth, and their opinion of it, in a quiet way, just set their poetical lathes a-turning, and twisted out ballads and songs for the good of the common cause."

In the compilation of this work, a few pieces have been included which do not strictly belong to the class of songs or ballads ; as in the case of the " Stamp Act Repeal," " Gentle Shepherd,"

" Burgoyne's Overthrow," etc. ; but their spirit and pertinency will, it is believed, justify their position as illustrative of the times and events to which they relate, in common with the other material of the work. The brief notes and illustrations to the different pieces in the collection which have been introduced, are intended to give, as far as practicable, accounts of their authorship, and to explain some of the more obscure allusions of the writers.

In conclusion the Editor acknowledges his obligations to the libraries of the New York Historical Society, of Yale College and Brown University, and especially to the officers of these institutions, for the facility with which he has been enabled to make use of their valuable collections. To Mr. J. CARTER BROWN of Providence, R. I., for access to his rich and unique collection on American history. To Col. PETER FORCE of Washington, for valuable aid and suggestions. To Mr. E. B.

CORWIN of New York, and the Rev. Dr. R W. GRISWOLD for similar favors—and though last, not least, for ready assistance and encouragement, to his brother, Mr. GEORGE H. MOORE, Librarian of the New York Historical Society.

NEW YORK, *December*, 1855.

CONTENTS.

———•♦•———

SONGS AND BALLADS.

————•♦•————

𝕋axation of 𝔄merica.

1765.

Peter St. John, the author of the following excellent ballad, was a native of Norwalk, Connecticut. During the early struggles of the Revolution, he kept a school in his native town, where he won much renown for the bold principles he avowed and inculcated. He wrote many pieces during the war, some of which are the finest of that period. At a later time he composed a poem entitled the "Death of Abel," in which are related "many things which might probably take place both before and after that barbarous fratricide."

AMERICAN TAXATION.[1]

WHILE I relate my story,
    Americans give ear;
Of Britain's fading glory
    You presently shall hear;

I'll give a true relation,
  Attend to what I say
Concerning the taxation
  Of North America.

The cruel lords of Britain,
  Who glory in their shame,
The project they have hit on
  They joyfully proclaim;
'Tis what they're striving after
  Our right to take away,
And rob us of our charter
  In North America.

There are two mighty speakers,
  Who rule in Parliament,
Who ever have been seeking
  Some mischief to invent;
'Twas North, and Bute his father,
  The horrid plan did lay
A mighty tax to gather
  In North America.

They searched the gloomy regions
　Of the infernal pit,
To find among their legions
　One who excelled in wit;
To ask of him assistance,
　Or tell them how they may
Subdue without resistance
　This North America.

Old Satan the arch traitor,
　Who rules the burning lake,
Where his chief navigator,
　Resolved a voyage to take;
For the Britannic ocean
　He launches far away,
To land he had no notion
　In North America.

He takes his seat in Britain,
　It was his soul's intent
Great George's throne to sit on,
　And rule the Parliament;

His comrades were pursuing
   A diabolic way,
For to complete the ruin
   Of North America.

He tried the art of magic
   To bring his schemes about,
At length the gloomy project
   He artfully found out;
The plan was long indulgèd
   In a clandestine way,
But lately was divulgèd
   In North America.

These subtle arch-combiners
   Addressed the British court,
All three were undersigners
   Of this obscure report—
There is a pleasant landscape
   That lieth far away
Beyond the wide Atlantic,
   In North America.

There is a wealthy people,
  Who sojourn in that land,
Their churches all with steeples
  Most delicately stand ;
Their houses like the gilly,
  Are painted red and gay :
They flourish like the lily
  In North America.

Their land with milk and honey,
  Continually doth flow,
The want of food or money
  They seldom ever know :
They heap up golden treasure,
  They have no debts to pay,
They spend their time in pleasure
  In North America.

On turkeys, fowls and fishes,
  Most frequently they dine,
With gold and silver dishes,
  Their tables always shine.

They crown their feasts with butter,
 They eat, and rise to play ;
In silks their ladies flutter,
 In North America.

With gold and silver laces
 They do themselves adorn,
The rubies deck their faces,
 Refulgent as the morn !
Wine sparkles in their glasses,
 They spend each happy day
In merriment and dances
 In North America.

Let not our suit affront you,
 When we address your throne,
O King, this wealthy country
 And subjects are your own,
And you, their rightful sovereign,
 They truly must obey,
You have a right to govern
 This North America.

O King, you've heard the sequel
　Of what we now subscribe,
Is it not just and equal
　To tax this wealthy tribe?
The question being askèd,
　His majesty did say,
My subjects shall be taxèd
　In North America.

Invested with a warrant,
　My publicans shall go,
The tenth of all their current
　They surely shall bestow;
If they indulge rebellion,
　Or from my precepts stray,
I'll send my war battalion
　To North America.

I'll rally all my forces
　By water and by land,
My light dragoons and horses
　Shall go at my command;

I'll burn both town and city,
　　With smoke becloud the day,
I'll show no human pity
　　For North America.

Go on, my hearty soldiers,
　　You need not fear of ill—
There's Hutchinson and Rogers,[2]
　　Their functions will fulfil—
They tell such ample stories,
　　Believe them sure we may,
One half of them are tories
　　In North America.

My gallant ships are ready
　　To waft you o'er the flood,
And in my cause be steady,
　　Which is supremely good;
Go ravage, steal and plunder,
　　And you shall have the prey;
They quickly will knock under
　　In North America.

The laws I have enacted,
　　I never will revoke,
Although they are neglected,
　　My fury to provoke.
I will forbear to flatter,
　　I'll rule the mighty sway,
I'll take away the charter
　　From North America.

O George! you are distracted,
　　You'll by experience find
The laws you have enacted
　　Are of the blackest kind.
I'll make a short digression,
　　And tell you by the way,
We fear not your oppression,
　　In North America.

Our fathers were distressèd,
　　While in their native land;
By tyrants were oppressèd
　　As we do understand;

For freedom and religion
  They were resolved to stray,
And trace the desert regions
  Of North America.

Heaven was their sole protector
  While on the roaring tide,
Kind fortune their director,
  And Providence their guide.
If I am not mistaken,
  About the first of May,
This voyage was undertaken
  For North America.

If rightly I remember,
  This country to explore,
They landed in November
  On Plymouth's desert shore.
The savages were nettled,
  With fear they fled away,
So peaceably they settled
  In North America.

We are their bold descendants,
  For liberty we'll fight,[3]
The claim to independence
  We challenge as our right;
'Tis what kind Heaven gave us,
  Who can it take away.
O, Heaven, sure will save us,
  In North America.

We never will knock under,
  O, George! we do not fear
The rattling of your thunder,
  Nor lightning of your spear:
Though rebels you declare us,
  We're strangers to dismay;
Therefore you cannot scare us
  In North America.

To what you have commanded
  We never will consent,
Although your troops are landed
  Upon our continent;

We'll take our swords and muskets,
And march in dread array,
And drive the British red-coats
From North America.

We have a bold commander,
Who fears not sword or gun,
The second Alexander,
His name is Washington.
His men are all collected,
And ready for the fray,
To fight they are directed
For North America.

We've Greene and Gates and Putnam
To manage in the field,
A gallant train of footmen,
Who'd rather die than yield;
A stately troop of horsemen
Train'd in a martial way,
For to augment our forces
In North America.

Proud George, you are engagèd
   All in a dirty cause,
A cruel war have wagèd
   Repugnant to all laws.
Go tell the savage nations
   You're crueler than they,
To fight your own relations
   In North America.

Ten millions you've expended,
   And twice ten millions more;
Our riches, you intended
   Should pay the mighty score.
Who now will stand your sponsor,
   Your charges to defray?
For sure you cannot conquer
   This North America.

I'll tell you, George, in metre,
   If you'll attend awhile;
We've forced your bold Sir Peter
   From Sullivan's fair isle.

At Monmouth, too, we gainèd
 The honors of the day—
The victory we obtainèd
 For North America.

Surely we were your betters
 Hard by the Brandywine;
We laid him fast in fetters
 Whose name was John Burgoyne;
We made your Howe to tremble
 With terror and dismay;
True heroes we resemble,
 In North America.

Confusion to the tories,
 That black infernal name,
In which Great Britain glories,
 For ever to her shame;
We'll send each foul revolter
 To smutty Africa,
Or noose him in a halter,
 In North America.

A health to our brave footmen,
    Who handle sword and gun,
To Greene and Gates and Putnam
    And conquering Washington;
Their names be wrote in letters
    Which never will decay,
While sun and moon do glitter
    On North America.

Success unto our allies
    In Holland, France and Spain,
Who man their ships and galleys,
    Our freedom to maintain;
May they subdue the rangers
    Of proud Britannia,
And drive them from their anchors
    In North America.

Success unto the Congress
    Of these United States,
Who glory in the conquests
    Of Washington and Gates;

To all, both land and seamen
    Who glory in the day
When we shall all be freemen
    In North America.

Success to legislation,
    That rules with gentle hand,
To trade and navigation,
    By water and by land.
May all with one opinion
    Our wholesome laws obey,
Throughout this vast dominion
    Of North America.

¹ " *Stamp Act*." On Monday, the 8th day of April, 1765, the ship
Edward arrived at New York, bringing the "terrible" news of the
passage of the Stamp Act. The people immediately declared their
determination to resist it, and the newspapers of the day declaimed
against it, saying "the account of these resolves must make the ears
of every American, who conceives himself to be a freeman, accord-
ing to the British constitution, to tingle, and fill him with astonishment." "The whole of the act is so artfully contrived and so
cautiously guarded, that there is no way to elude the design of it,
but by rejecting the whole as an unconstitutional attempt upon our
liberties, and by nobly opposing every effort that may be made to
put it in execution."

² " *There's Hutchinson and Rogers.* This probably refers to Jere-
miah Dummer Rogers, one of the barristers and attorneys who

were addressers of Governor Hutchinson, on his departure for England in 1774. After the battle of Breed's Hill, he took refuge in Boston, and was appointed commissary to the royal troops that continued to occupy Charlestown. At the evacuation of Boston in 1776, he accompanied the royal army to Halifax, where he died in 1784.

Sabine's Amer. Loyalists.

3 *For Liberty we'll fight.* " *Liberty, Property,* and No Stamps," was " the united voice of all His Majesty's *free* and *loyal* subjects in America." The following verses appeared during the excitement caused by the " odious act," accompanied with the remark that "the stanzas are indeed not very poetical ; but there is no doubt the zeal of the author for the cause of liberty will atone for publishing the laudable attempts of an unpractised muse."

> Cursed be the man who e'er shall raise
> His sacrilegious hand,
> To drive fair liberty, our praise !
> From his own native land.
>
> O may his memory never die,
> By future ages curst ;
> But live to lasting infamy,
> Branded of traytor's worth.
>
> But happy ! happy ! happy they,
> Who in their country's cause
> Shall cast reluctant fear away,
> Immortal in applause !
>
> Who with their conscious virtue girt,
> Shan't dread oppression's voice ;
> But boldly dare those rights t' assert,
> In which all men rejoice.

Holt's Gazette, No. 1169.

Liberty Tree.

1765.

This beautiful ballad was written by Thomas Paine, the author of " The Age of Reason," and published in the Pennsylvania Magazine of July, 1775, while he was editor of that periodical. He composed and published many songs and elegies during his connection with the Magazine. Among them " The Death of Wolfe, on the plains of Abraham," is uncommonly pathetic and graceful.

LIBERTY TREE.

In a chariot of light from the regions of day,
    The Goddess of Liberty came ;
Ten thousand celestials directed the way,
    And hither conducted the dame.
A fair budding branch from the gardens above,
    Where millions with millions agree,
She brought in her hand as a pledge of her love,
    And the plant she named *Liberty Tree.*[3]

The celestial exotic struck deep in the ground,
   Like a native it flourish'd and bore ;
The fame of its fruit drew the nations around,
   To seek out this peaceable shore.
Unmindful of names or distinctions they came,
   For freemen like brothers agree ;
With one spirit endued, they one friendship pursued,
   And their temple was *Liberty Tree.*

Beneath this fair tree, like the patriarchs of old,
   Their bread in contentment they ate
Unvex'd with the troubles of silver and gold,
   The cares of the grand and the great.
With timber and tar they Old England supply'd,
   And supported her pow'r on the sea ;
Her battles they fought, without getting a groat,
   For the honor of *Liberty Tree.*

But hear, O ye swains, 'tis a tale most profane,
   How all the tyrannical powers,
Kings, Commons and Lords, are uniting amain,
   To cut down this guardian of ours ;

From the east to the west blow the trumpet to arms,

Thro' the land let the sound of it flee,

Let the far and the near, all unite with a cheer,

In defence of our *Liberty Tree.*

[1] *Liberty Tree.* During the Stamp Act excitement there arose a practice of signifying public sentiment in a very effectual way; though without any responsible agent, unless the inanimate Liberty Tree may be so considered. This tree was a majestic elm that stood in front of a house opposite the Boylston market, on the edge of the "High street," in the town of Boston. On the 14th of August, 1765, an effigy representing Andrew Oliver, a gentleman appointed to distribute the stamps, was found hanging upon this tree, with a paper before it, on which was written in large characters,

> " Fair freedom's glorious cause I've meanly quitted,
>   For the sake of pelf;
> But ah! the Devil has me outwitted,
> And instead of *stamping* others, I've *hang'd* myself.

" P. S. Whoever takes this down is an enemy to his country.'
On the right arm was written " A. O." and on the left,

> " What greater pleasure can there be,
> Than to see a *stamp man* hanging on a tree ! "

On another part of the tree a *boot* was suspended : the emblem of the Earl of Bute, first Lord of the Treasury, from which the devil, with the Stamp Act in his hand, was looking out. Chief Justice (afterwards governor) Hutchinson, directed the sheriff to remove this exhibition, but his deputies, from a fear of the popular feeling, declined. In the evening the figures were taken down by the people and carried in procession through the streets. After demolishing the stamp-office, in State street, they proceeded to Fort

Hill, where a bonfire was made of the pageantry in sight of Mr. Oliver's house. It being intimated to Mr. Oliver that it would conduce to the quiet of the public, if he would go to the tree and openly resign his commission, he appeared the next day, and declared, in the presence of a large concourse of people, that he would not continue in office. It was thenceforward called the *Liberty Tree*, and the following inscription was placed upon it, " *This tree was planted in the year* 1614, *and pruned by the order of the Sons of Liberty, February* 14, 1766." On future occasions there was seldom any excitement on political subjects, without some evidence of it appearing on this tree. Whenever obnoxious offices were to be resigned or agreements for patriotic purposes entered into, the parties were notified to appear at the tree, " where they always found pens and paper, and a numerous crowd of witnesses, though the genius of the tree was invisible. When the British army took possession of Boston, in 1774, Liberty Tree fell a victim to their vengeance, or to that of the persons to whom its shade had been disagreeable." Liberty Trees were consecrated in Charlestown, Lexington and Roxbury, Mass., and also in Charleston, S. C., Newport and Providence, R. I.—*Tudor's Life of Otis*

The Repeal.

1766.

The Stamp Act was passed on the tenth of January, 1765, and repealed on the twenty-second of February, of the next year. The news of its repeal was hailed with joy. Bonfires illuminated the hills, and the voice of the people throughout the country united in one earnest display of exultation and loyalty. Many pieces, both in prose and metre, appeared at the time, celebrating the occasion. The following is declared, in the papers of the day, to have been spoken at "a mirthful celebration of the *free* inhabitants of Northampton, Virginia."

STAMP ACT REPEAL.

In Greece and Rome renowned for art and arms,
Whose every bosom felt fair Freedom's charms,
Those manly breasts which generous ardor fired,
When public weal their swords or care required;
When peace abroad their conquering arms procured,
At home, when wisdom, Liberty secured:

Greatly unbending o'er the social bowl,
Indulged the transports of a genial soul.
So we, nor second to those sons of Fame,
In love of freedom, tho' of humbler name;
Or dauntless courage, bravely to oppose
Domestic tyranny, or foreign foes;—
We, who far foremost *here*, a virtuous few,
Dare to our country and ourselves be true;
Who dare, in spite of ev'ry venal frown,
Assert our rights, and lawless power disown;
Spite of each parasite, each cringing slave,
Each cautious dastard, each oppressive knave;
Each gibing Ass, *that reptile of an hour*,
The supercilious pimp of abject slaves in power;
Spite of those empty boasters, who conceal
Their coward fear with circumspection's veil,
Are met, to celebrate in festive mirth
The day that gives our *second* freedom birth;
That tells us, *Britain's Grenvilles* never more
Shall dare usurp unjust, illegal power,
Or threat *America's* free sons with chains,
While the least spark of ancient fire remains;
While records bid the virtuous sons admire
The godlike acts of each intrepid sire.

Exult *America !* each dauntless son
Will ever keep fair Liberty their own ;
Will base submission, servile fear despise,
And Freedom's *substance*, not her *shadow* prize.
Triumph America ! thy patriot voice
Has made the greatest of mankind rejoice,
Immortal PITT !—O ever glorious name !
Far, far unequalled in the rolls of fame !
What breast, for virtue is by all approved,
And freedom even by Asia's slaves beloved,—
What breast but glows with gratitude to thee,
Boast of mankind, great prop of Liberty !
To thee, the best of parents and of friends,
America with grateful homage bends,
Her thanks, her love, unable to express,
To thee, great patron of her happiness.
Raised by thy hand, beneath thy guardian care,
Luxuriant blooms adorn her vernal year ;
And, when rapacious harpies would devour
The infant fruit, and blast the tender flower,
Shielded by thee, she mocks the abortive wiles ;
Beneath thy shade, again her verdure smiles.

Would 'twere in pity to mankind decreed,
That still a PITT should to a PITT succeed :

When proud oppression would subvert the laws,
That still a CAMDEN should defend the cause.
Nor let's forget the gallant BARRE's merit,
His TULLY's periods and his CATO's spirit;
His, too, an honest independent heart,
Where fear, nor fraud, nor avarice have part:
Or generous MEREDITH, our worthy friend,
The first our injured freedom to defend;
Who nobly, not by powerful wrath deterred,
Our just remonstrance and complaints preferred.

    Proceed, great names! your mighty influence join,
Your country's arts, and policies refine:
Assist great CONWAY, and reform the state;
Bid peaceful commerce reassume her seat;
Bid BRITISH navies whiten ev'ry coast,
And BRITISH freedom ev'ry country boast.
Let us then, emulous of each great name
Conspicuous in the ancient page of fame,
Resolve, that freedom to our sons be sped,
Not worse than when our valiant fathers bled:
Emerging glorious from our late distress,
Let ev'ry bosom hail returning peace:
This day let nought but jocund mirth employ,
Relax each brow, and give a loose to joy.

    2

And you, ye fair, on whom our hopes depend,
Our future fame and empire to extend;
Whose fruitful beds will dauntless myriads yield,
To fight for freedom in some future field;
Resign each fear.

To-day, let gladness beam in every face,
Soften each smile and brighten every grace;
While the glad roofs with lofty notes resound,
With grace harmonious move the mazy round.
Make our hearts feel the long-forgotten fire
Wake into flame each spark of soft desire.
Too long indignant tumults and alarms
Have made us heedless of your lovely charms:
But, now, beneath the downy wings of peace,
With freedom blest, our care shall be to please;
Each day the genial pleasure to improve,
And add new sweetness to connubial love.

The Gentle Shepherd.

1766.

THE incident which gave rise to the following satirical parody of Pope's second pastoral, occurred during the debates in Parliament early in the year 1766, which took place on occasion of the repeal of the famous Cider-tax, a measure which gave to the inhabitants of the cider-counties a "taste of the same pleasure, which their brethren in America about the same time enjoyed" in the repeal of the Stamp Act. George Grenville, then leader in the Commons, came to the rescue of Bute, Chancellor of the Exchequer, and spoke strongly on his favorite theme, the profusion with which the late war had been carried on. That profusion, he said, had made taxes necessary. He called on the gentleman opposite to him to say where they would have a tax laid, and dwelt on this topic with his usual prolixity. "Let them tell me where," he repeated in a monotonous and somewhat fretful tone. "I say, sir, let them tell me where. I repeat it, sir, I am entitled to say to them, Tell me where." Unluckily for him, Pitt had come down to the House that night, and nad been bitterly provoked by the reflections thrown on the war. He revenged himself by murmuring in a whine resembling Grenville's, a line of a well-known song, " Gentle Shepherd, tell me where." "If," cried Grenville, " gentlemen are to be treated in this way—" Pitt, as was his fashion, when he meant to mark extreme contempt, rose deliberately, made his bow, and walked out of the House, leaving his brother-in-law in convulsions of rage, and every body else in convulsions of laughter. It was long before Grenville lost the nickname of " Gentle Shepherd."[1]

THE GENTLE SHEPHERD.

A GENTLE SHEPHERD—that's his proper name—
Retired to Stow, far distant from the Thame;
Where dancing fishes in the basin play'd,
And crowded columns form'd a marble shade:
There, while he mourn'd by streams that never flow,
The statues round a dumb compassion show;
The worthies listen'd in each sculptur'd hall;
My Lord, consenting, sat and heard it all.

Ye stubborn York, ye fierce New England crew,
Free from Excise, but not from Customs too,
To you I mourn, nor to the deaf I sing,
Your woods shall answer, and your cities ring.
Quebec and Georgia, my stamp duties pay;
Why are you prouder, and more hard than they ?

The gay Creoles, with my new tax agree,
They parch'd by heat, and I inflam'd by thee;
The sultry Sirius burns their sugar-canes,
While in thy heart a wholesome winter reigns.

Where stray ye, members, in what lane or grove,
While to enforce the act I hopeless move?
In those fair rooms where Royal G—— resides,
Or where the Cockpit's ample hall divides,
As in the gilded sconce I view my face,
No rising blushes stain the faithful glass;
But since my figure pleases there no more,
I shun the levee which I sought before.
Once I was skill'd in every fund that went,
From India bonds to humble cent per cent.
Ah, Gentle Shepherd, what avails thy skill
To frame a tax for D—w—ll to repeal?

Let —— proud preside at C——l B——d,
Or wily H—l—d still desire to hoard;
But in the Treasury let me spend *my* days,
And load the sinking fund a thousand ways.
That wand was mine, which B——, with panting breath,
Into my hands, resigning, did bequeath:

He said, G—— G——v——le, take this rod, the same
That to the cider counties taught my name;
But R—k—ham may sway the wand for me,
Since I'm despisèd and disgrac'd by thee.
Oh! were I made, by some transforming power,
The smooth-tongued P—— that speaks in yonder bower,
Then might my voice the listening ears employ,
And I, the pension he receives, enjoy.

   And yet my speeches pleased the Tory throng,
Rough R—gby grinn'd, and N—l—n prais'd my song;
The Cits, while Bow church bells forgot to ring,
In milk white wigs, their kind addresses bring.
But their addresses are preferred in vain,
On P——t their thanks are now bestow'd again:
For him the richest boxes are designed,
And in one parchment all their freedom's join'd.
Accept their wreaths, allow your partners none,
Claim all their praise as due to you alone.

   See what strange things in the repeal appear;
Discordant Earls have form'd a union here:
In opposition B—— and T—p—e join,
And wicked Twitcher[2] with good ——.
Come, matchless Jemmy! bless the cool retreats,
When Peers from voting quit their scarlet seats;

When weary Commons leave the sultry town,
And, drown'd with debts, to finger rents go down.
This harmless grove no lurking bailiff hides,
But in my breast the serpent *rage* abides.
Oh, how I long with you to pass my days,
Drink our own healths, and sound each other's praise;
Your praise the press shall bear through all the town,
And evening posts from London waft it down :
But would you write, and rival Anti's strain,
The wondering mob his lies would read again;
The moving carman hear the powerful call,
And pots of beer hang listening in their fall.

But see, the ladies shun the noontide air,
And hungry Lords to dinner fast repair :
At table all to places fix'd resort—
Ye gods, and is there then no place at court ?
But soon the sun with milder rays descends
To western climes, where my stamp duty ends :
On my poor effigy[3] their furies prey,
By night they burn me, as they hang by day.

[1] Earl of Chatham; an Essay by Thos. Babington Macaulay, 1844.

[2] *And wicked Twitcher.* Lord Sandwich was universally known by the sobriquet of "Jemmy Twitcher."

[3] *On my poor effigy.* Effigies of the different members of the Min-

istry were carted through the principal places in the Colonies, to conspicuous situations, and there burned. The people could not degrade such " perverters of the public weal" sufficiently. Epigrams, pasquinades and scurrilous verses appeared at every corner in " flaming capitals," and Britain's dishonor was published from the pulpit. The following appeared, suspended upon Liberty Tree, during Grenville's official career :

" Pitt, the supporter of Liberty and the terror of tyrants."

> " To Bute and Grenville, mark the event,
>   Both heaven and earth are foes;
> While curses on each wretch are sent
>   By every wind that blows."
>   *God save the King.*

The Old Woman Taught Wisdom.

1767.

The ballad entitled "The World Turned Upside Down, or, The Old Woman Taught Wisdom," was published, originally, in the Gentleman's Magazine, and afterwards on a music-sheet, set to the tune, "Derry Down." The anonymous author, says, it is "an humble attempt to reconcile the parent and her children, made by a peacemaker to Great Britain and her Colonies."

THE WORLD TURNED UPSIDE DOWN.

Goody Bull and her daughter together fell out,
Both squabbled, and wrangled, and made a —— rout,
But the cause of the quarrel remains to be told,
Then lend both your ears, and a tale I'll unfold.

The old lady, it seems, took a freak in her head,
That her daughter, grown woman, might earn her own
    bread:

    2*

Self-applauding her scheme, she was ready to dance;
But we're often too sanguine in what we advance.

For mark the event; thus by fortune we're crossed,
Nor should people reckon without their good host;
The daughter was sulky, and wouldn't come to,
And pray, what in this case could the old woman do?

In vain did the matron hold forth in the cause,
That the young one was able; her duty, the laws;
Ingratitude vile, disobedience far worse;
But she might e'en as well sung psalms to a horse.

Young, froward, and sullen, and vain of her beauty,
She tartly replied, that she knew well her duty,
That other folks' children were kept by their friends,
And that some folks loved people but for their own ends.

Zounds, neighbor! quoth Pitt, what the devil's the matter?
A man cannot rest in his house for your clatter;
Alas! cries the daughter, here's dainty fine work,
The old woman grown harder than Jew or than Turk.

She be ———, says the farmer, and to her he goes,
First roars in her ears, then tweaks her old nose,
Hallo, Goody, what ails you? Wake! woman, I say;
I am come to make peace, in this desperate fray.

Adzooks, ope thine eyes, what a pother is here!
You've no right to compel her, you have not, I swear;
Be ruled by your friends, kneel down and ask pardon,
You'd be sorry, I'm sure, should she walk Covent Garden.

Alas! cries the old woman, and must I comply?
But I'd rather submit than the huzzy should die;
Pooh, prithee be quiet, be friends and agree,
You must surely be right, *if you're guided by me.*

Unwillingly awkward, the mother knelt down,
While the absolute farmer went on with a frown,
Come, kiss the poor child, there come, kiss and be friends!
There, kiss your poor daughter, and make her amends.

No thanks to you, mother; the daughter replied:
But thanks to my friend here, I've humbled your pride.

The Liberty Song.

1768.

A short time after the refusal of the Massachusetts Legislature to rescind the Circular Letter of February 11, 1768, relating to the imposition of duties and taxes on the American colonies, John Dickinson[1] of Delaware, the celebrated author of a series of essays entitled "The Farmer's Letters," wrote to James Otis of Massachusetts, as follows: "I enclose you a song for American freedom. I have long since renounced poetry, but as indifferent songs are very powerful on certain occasions, I venture to invoke the deserted muses. I hope my good intentions will procure pardon, with those I wish to please, for the boldness of my numbers. My worthy friend, Dr. Arthur Lee,[2] a gentleman of distinguished family, abilities and patriotism, in Virginia, composed eight lines of it. Cardinal De Retz always enforced his political operations by songs. I wish our attempt may be useful." This song was published in the Boston Gazette of July 18, 1768, to which paper Mr. Otis, and other early advocates of political and religious liberty, often contributed. It also appeared in the various newspapers of New England, where it soon became very popular.

On the sixth of July, two days after the date of his first letter, Mr. Dickinson wrote again to Mr. Otis, saying, "I enclosed you the other day a copy of a song composed in great haste. I think it was rather too bold. I now send a corrected copy which I like better. If you think the bagatelle worth publishing, I beg it may be this copy. If the first is published before this is come to hand, I shall be much obliged to you if you will be so good as to publish this with some little note, 'that this is the true copy of the original.' [3] In this copy I think it may be well enough to add between the fourth and fifth stanzas these lines:

> *How sweet are the labors that freemen endure,*
> *That they shall enjoy all the profit, secure—*
> *No more such sweet labors Americans know,*
> *If Britons shall reap what Americans sow.*
> *In freedom we're born—"*

A SONG NOW MUCH IN VOGUE IN NORTH AMERICA.

1768.

COME join hand in hand, brave Americans all,
And rouse your bold hearts at fair Liberty's call;
No tyrannous acts, shall suppress your just claim,
Or stain with dishonor America's name.
  In freedom we're born, and in freedom we'll live;
      Our purses are ready,
      Steady, Friends, steady,
  Not as *slaves*, but as *freemen* our money we'll give.

Our worthy forefathers—let's give them a cheer—
To climates unknown did courageously steer;
Thro' oceans to deserts, for freedom they came,
And, dying, bequeath'd us their freedom and fame.

Their generous bosoms all dangers despis'd,
So highly, so wisely, their birthrights they priz'd;
We'll keep what they gave, we will piously keep,
Nor frustrate their toils on the land or the deep.

The Tree, their own hands had to Liberty rear'd,
They lived to behold growing strong and rever'd;
With transport then cried,—" Now our wishes we gain,
For our children shall gather the fruits of our pain. "

How sweet are the labors that freemen endure,
That they shall enjoy all the profit, secure,—
No more such sweet labors Americans know,
If Britons shall reap what Americans sow.

Swarms of placemen and pensioners [4] soon will appear,
Like locusts deforming the charms of the year:
Suns vainly will rise, showers vainly descend,
If we are to drudge for what others shall spend.

Then join hand in hand brave Americans all,
By uniting we stand, by dividing we fall;
In so righteous a cause let us hope to succeed,
For Heaven approves of each generous deed.

All ages shall speak with amaze and applause,
Of the courage we'll show in support of our laws;
To die we can bear,—but to serve we disdain,
For shame is to freemen more dreadful than pain.

This bumper I crown for our sovereign's health,
And this for Britannia's glory and wealth;
That wealth, and that glory immortal may be,
If she is but just, and we are but free.

　　In freedom we're born, &c.

[1] *John Dickinson* occupies a prominent position in the early history of the Revolution. He was a member of the Pennsylvania Assembly in 1764; of the Congress of 1765, and also of the first Continental Congress, which met in Carpenter's Hall at Philadelphia on
the fourth of September, 1774. Of the important and eloquent state
papers of that Congress, he wrote the principal part. Though so
little a republican at the commencement of the Revolutionary difficulties, as to oppose the Declaration of Independence, because he
doubted the policy of Congress, " without some preclusory trials of
our strength," he fully proved the sincerity of his attachment to the

liberties of his country by marching to Elizabethtown, at the head of his regiment, a short time after the declaration, to repel the invading enemy. In November, 1767, the first of a series of communications written by him, entitled " Letters from a farmer in Pennsylvania, to the inhabitants of the British Colonies," appeared in the Pennsylvania Chronicle. Dickinson died February 14, 1808.

[2] *Arthur Lee* was a bold and fearless patriot. At the commencement of the troubles with the mother country, he went to England, from whence he rendered most important services to his country, by sending to the patriots the earliest intelligence of the plans of the Ministry. His writings are numerous, chiefly political ; among them the most celebrated, are the letters under the signature of " Junius Americanus." In a letter to Samuel Adams he says, " The first wish of my heart is, that America may be free—the second is—that we may ever be united with this country. But this union, however desirable, must not be upon dishonorable and slavish terms."

[3] In the Pennsylvania Chronicle, published at Philadelphia, July 4 –11, 1768, this amended copy appears ; but we do not find it complete in any of the Boston papers. It is probable that the request of the author was never complied with, and if there was any alteration in the copy published after July 18, it was done without any note or comment. Late in September, it appeared in a ballad sheet, set to the majestic air, " Hearts of Oak," and was sung in the streets of Boston and the villages of New England, by all the sons of freedom, who " promised themselves that all ages would applaud their courage."

[4] *Swarms of placemen and pensioners.* The Ministry have already begun to give away in pensions the money they lately took out of our pockets, *without our leave.—Note by the author of the song.*

A Parody

UPON A WELL-KNOWN LIBERTY SONG.

1768.

This parody, upon the preceding song, was first published in the Boston Gazette, on the twenty-sixth of September, 1768, with the subjoined brief notice. "Last Tuesday, the following song made its appearance from a garret at Castle William." The author is unknown.

THE PARODY.

COME shake your dull noddles, ye pumpkins, and bawl,
And own that you're mad at fair Liberty's call;
No scandalous conduct can add to your shame,
Condemn'd to dishonor, inherit the fame.
 In folly you're born, and in folly you'll live,
   To madness still ready,
   And stupidly steady,
 Not as men, but as monkeys, the tokens you give.

Your grandsire, old Satan, now give him a cheer,
Would act like yourselves, and as wildly would steer :
So great an example in prospect still keep,
Whilst you are alive, Old Belza may sleep.

Such villains, such rascals, all dangers despise,
And stick not at mobbing when mischief's the prize;
They burst thro' all barriers, and piously keep
Such chattels and goods the vile rascals can sweep.

The Tree, which the wisdom of justice hath rear'd,
Should be stout for their use, and by no means be spar'd :
When fuddled with rum the mad sots to restrain,
Sure Tyburn will sober the wretches again.

Your brats and your bunters by no means forget,
But feather your nests, for they're bare enough yet;
From the insolent rich sure the poor knave may steal,
Who ne'er in his life knew the scent of a meal.

When in your own cellars you've quaff'd a regale,
Then drive, tug and ——, the next house to assail;
For short is your harvest, nor long shall you know
The pleasure of reaping what other men sow.

Then plunder, my lads, for when red coats appear,
You'll melt like the locust when winter is near;
Gold vainly will glow, silver vainly will shine,
But, faith, you must skulk, you no more shall purloin.

Then nod your poor numskulls, ye pumpkins, and bawl,
The de'il take such rascals, fools, whoresons and all;
Your cursèd old trade of purloining must cease,
The dread and the curse of all order and peace.

All ages shall speak with contempt and amaze,
Of the vilest banditti that swarm'd in these days;
In defiance of halters, of whips and of chains,
The rogues would run riot,—fools for their pains.

Gulp down your last dram, for the gallows now groans,
And, over depress'd, her lost empire bemoans;
While we quite transported and happy shall be,
From mobs, knaves and villains, protected and free

The Parody Parodised.

MASSACHUSETTS LIBERTY SONG.

1768.

This loyal song is much the best of those composed during the earliest struggles of the Colonists, and is forcibly illustrative of the nature and spirit of the times in which it was composed. It was published in the St. James Chronicle, at London, on the eighth of November, 1768, as well as in America, and intended as a rejoinder to the foregoing parody.

THE PARODY PARODISED.

COME swallow your bumpers, ye tories, and roar,
That the sons of fair Freedom are hamper'd once more;
But know that no cut-throats our spirits can tame,
Nor a host of oppressors shall smother the flame.

In freedom we're born, and, like sons of the brave,
  We'll never surrender,
  But swear to defend her,
And scorn to survive, if unable to save.

Our grandsires, blest heroes! we'll give them a tear,
Nor sully their honors, by stooping to fear;
Thro' deaths and thro' dangers, their trophies they won,
We dare be their rivals, nor will be outdone.

Let tyrants and minions presume to despise,
Encroach on our rights, and make freedom their prize:
The fruits of their rapine they never shall keep;
Tho' vengeance may nod, yet how short is her sleep!

The tree, which proud Haman for Mordecai rear'd,
Stands recorded, that virtue endanger'd is spar'd,
That rogues whom no bonds and no laws can restrain,
Must be stript of their honors, and humbled again.

Our wives and our babes, still protected, shall know,
Those who dare to be free, shall for ever be so;
On these arms and these hearts they may safely rely,
For in freedom we'll live, or like heroes we'll die.

Ye insolent tyrants! who wish to enthrall
Ye minions, ye placemen, pimps, pensioners, all,
How short is your triumph! how feeble your trust!
Your honors must wither and nod to the dust.

When oppress'd and reproach'd, our king we implore,
Still firmly persuaded our rights he'll restore;
When our hearts beat to arms, to defend a just right,
Our monarch rules there, and forbids us to fight.

Not the glitter of arms, nor the dread of a fray,
Could make us submit to their chains for a day;
Withheld by affection, on Britons we call,—
Prevent the fierce conflict which threatens your fall!

All ages shall speak, with amaze and applause,
Of the prudence we show in support of our cause;
Assur'd of our safety, a Brunswick still reigns,
Whose free loyal subjects are strangers to chains.

Then join hand in hand, brave Americans all!
To be free is to live, to be slaves is to fall;
Has the land such a dastard, as scorns not a lord,
Who dreads not a fetter much more than a sword.

In freedom we're born, and, like sons of the brave,
  We'll never surrender,
  But swear to defend her,
And scorn to survive, if unable to save.

Hearts of Oak. The original song, under this title, was composed by David Garrick. It was very popular during the American wars, both of 1776 and 1812, among the British, and at the present day is sung by many of

    " Our soldiers, our sailors, our statesmen,"

in " merrie old England."

To the Ladies.

1769.

In the year 1768, the people of Boston resolved that they would not import any tea, glass, paper, or other commodities commonly brought from Great Britain, until the act imposing duties upon all such articles should be repealed. This poetical appeal to the ladies of the country, to lend a "helping hand" for the furtherance of that resolution, appeared in the Boston News Letter, anonymously.

TO OUR LADIES.

Young ladies in town, and those that live round,
  Let a friend at this season advise you;
Since money's so scarce, and times growing worse,
  Strange things may soon hap and surprise you.

First, then, throw aside your topknots of pride;
 Wear none but your own country linen;
Of economy boast, let your pride be the most
 To show clothes of your own make and spinning.[1]

What if homespun they say is not quite so gay
 As brocades, yet be not in a passion,
For when once it is known this is much worn in town,
 One and all will cry out—'Tis the fashion !

And, as one, all agree, that you'll not married be
 To such as will wear London factory,
But at first sight refuse, tell 'em such you will choose
 As encourage our own manufactory.

No more ribbons wear, nor in rich silks appear;
 Love your country much better than fine things;
Begin without passion, 'twill soon be the fashion
 To grace your smooth locks with a twine string.

Throw aside your Bohea, and your Green Hyson tea,
 And all things with a new-fashion duty;
Procure a good store of the choice Labrador,
 For there'll soon be enough here to suit you.

 3

These do without fear, and to all you'll appear,

    Fair, charming, true, lovely and clever;

Though the times remain darkish, young men may be
    sparkish,

    And love you much stronger than ever.

Then make yourselves easy, for no one will teaze ye,

    Nor *tax* you, if chancing to sneer

At the sense-ridden tools, who think us all fools;

    But they'll find the reverse far and near.

[1] *To show clothes of your own make and spinning.* About this time
a party of young ladies, calling themselves "Daughters of Liberty,"
met at the house of "a distinguished minister, in Boston, where
they amused themselves with spinning two hundred and thirty-two
skeins of yarn, some very fine, which were given to the worthy
pastor, several of the party being members of his congregation.
The party was concluded with many agreeable tunes, anthems and
liberty songs, with great judgment; fine voices performing, which
were animated, in all their several parts, by a number of the Sons
of Liberty." The following quotation, from Murray's United States,
shows the effect such resolutions and actions had upon the trade of
England with the Colonies. The exports from England, which, "in
1768 amounted to $11,890,000, declined, in 1769, to $8,170,000."

A New Song.

1770.

These verses appeared in a broadside, a short time after the
" massacre of the fifth of March,"[1] 1770, as a " new song much in
vogue among the friends to arbitary power, and the soldiery at Castle Island,[2] where it was composed, since the troops have evacuated
the town of Boston."

CASTLE ISLAND SONG.

You simple Bostonians, I'd have you beware,
Of your Liberty Tree, I would have you take care,
For if that we chance to return to the town,
Your houses and stores will come tumbling down.

 Derry down, down, hey derry down.

If you will not agree to Old England's laws,
I fear that King Hancock will soon get the *yaws :*
But he need not fear, for I swear we will,
For the want of a doctor give him a hard pill.

A brave reinforcement, we soon think to get;
Then we will make you poor pumpkins to sweat :
Our drums they'll rattle, and then you will run
To the devil himself, from the sight of a gun.

Our fleet and our army, they soon will arrive,
Then to a bleak island, you shall not us drive.
In every house, you shall have three or four,
And if that will not please you, you shall have half a score.

 Derry down, down, hey derry down.

[1] *Massacre of the fifth of March.* Two regiments of British troops
under command of Colonels Dalrymple and Carr, arrived at Boston
in the month of September, 1768. The people of Boston desired
that they should be stationed at the Castle, but "they landed with
all the appearance of hostility! They marched through the town
with all the ensigns of triumph, evidently designed to subject the
inhabitants to the severe discipline of a garrison, and continued their
enormities by abusing the people." On the second day of March,
1770, a quarrel arose between two soldiers of the 29th regiment,
and the workmen at a ropewalk not far distant from the barracks.
The soldiers being repulsed, soon made another attack, having in-

creased their number to ten or twelve, but these were also success-
fully resisted. In consequence of these quarrels the soldiery declared
they would be avenged. The following account of their proceedings
is taken from the Boston Chronicle of March 8, 1770. "Last Monday about 9 o'clock at night a most unfortunate affair happened in
King Street. The sentinel posted at the Custom House, being surrounded by a number of people, called to the main-guard, upon which
Captain Preston, with a party, went to his assistance, soon after
which some of the party fired, by which the following persons were
killed. Samuel Gray, rope maker, a mulatto man, named Attucks,
and Mr. James Caldwell. Early the next morning Captain Preston
was committed to jail, and the same day eight soldiers. A meeting
of the inhabitants was called at Faneuil Hall that forenoon, and the
lieutenant-governor and council met at the council chamber,
where the Colonels, Dalrymple and Carr, were desired to attend,
when it was concluded upon, that both regiments should go down to
the barracks at Castle William, as soon as they were ready to receive
them."

The funeral of the victims of the massacre was attended the 8th
of March. On this occasion the shops of the town were closed, and
all the bells were ordered to be tolled, as were those of the neighboring towns. The procession began to move between 4 and 5
o'clock, P. M., the bodies of the two strangers, *Caldwell* and *Attucks*,
being borne from Faneuil Hall, and those of the other victims, from
the residence of their families,—the hearses meeting in King Street,
near the scene of the tragedy, and passing through the main street,
to the burial ground, where the bodies were all deposited in one
vault. Patrick Carr, who was wounded in the affair, died on the
14th, and was buried on the 17th, in the same vault with his mur-
dered associates. Shortly after the occurrence Paul Revere, of Boston, engraved and printed a large handbill, giving a sketch of the
scene, and accompanied it with the following lines :

> " Unhappy Boston ! see thy sons deplore
> Thy hallowed walks besmear'd with guiltless gore.

> While faithless Preston and his savage bands,
> With murderous rancor stretch their bloody hands;
> Like fierce barbarians grinning o'er their prey,
> Approve the carnage and enjoy the day.
> If scalding drops, from rage, from anguish wrung,
> If speechless sorrows lab'ring for a tongue .
> Or if a weeping world can aught appease
> The plaintive ghosts of victims such as these ;
> The patriot's copious tears for each are shed,
> A glorious tribute which embalms the dead.
> But know, Fate summons to that awful goal,
> Where justice strips the murderer of his soul:
> Should venal C—ts, the scandal of the land,
> Snatch the relentless villain from her hand,
> Keen execrations on this plate inscrib'd
> Shall reach a judge who never can be bribed."

[2] *Castle Island.* Castle William was situated on this island. In 1798, the fortress was ceded to the United States, and in the following year was named by President Adams, *Fort Independence.*

The Taxed Tea.

1773.

On the tenth day of May, 1773, the East India Company were authorized, by act of Parliament, to export their tea, free of duty, to England, but with a tax of threepence a pound to all ports in the American Colonies. This was considered by the colonists as a scheme of the Ministry to prepare them for an unlimited taxation. Advice having been received, that the company had resolved to send out large quantities of tea on their own account, to be sold in the various colonies, the people immediately resolved to send it back to England, in the same ships in which it should come. The pilots were directed how to proceed with the ships on their arrival, and were required to bring them no farther than within the entrance of the harbor. The consignees were summoned to appear at Liberty Tree and resign their office ; but to this they replied in letters "daringly affrontive to the town," declining to resign. On the morning of the twenty-eighth of November, the ship Dartmouth, with one hundred and fourteen chests of the long-expected tea, came to anchor near the Castle in Boston harbor, and on the following morning came up and anchored off Griffin's wharf. At the same time, near seven thousand persons, from the several towns around Boston, "respectable for their ranks and abilities, and venerable for their age and character," assembled and unanimously adhered to their former resolution, that the tea should not be landed. "During the session of this meeting, a number of persons, disguised as Indians, approached near to the door of the Assembly, and gave the war-whoop, which was answered by a few in the galleries of the house. The savages then repaired to the ships [now numbering three], which harbored the pestilential teas, and began their ravage. They applied themselves in earnest, and in about two hours, broke up three hundred and forty-two chests of tea and discharged their contents into the sea." This song appeared a short time after the occurrence, in the Pennsylvania Packet, under the name of "A new Song, to the plaintive tune of 'Hozier's Ghost.'"

A NEW SONG.

As near beauteous Boston lying,
  On the gently swelling flood,
Without jack or pendant flying,
  Three ill-fated tea-ships rode.

Just as glorious Sol was setting,
  On the wharf, a numerous crew,
Sons of freedom, fear forgetting,
  Suddenly appeared in view.

Armed with hammers, axe and chisels,
  Weapons new for warlike deed,
Towards the herbage-freighted vessels,
  They approached with dreadful speed.

O'er their heads aloft in mid-sky,
  Three bright angel forms were seen;
This was Hampden, that was Sidney,
  With fair Liberty between.

"Soon," they cried, "your foes you'll banish,
  Soon the triumph shall be won;
Scarce shall setting Phœbus vanish,
  Ere the deathless deed be done." [1]

Quick as thought the ships were boarded,
  Hatches burst and chests displayed;
Axes, hammers help afforded;
  What a glorious crash they made.

Squash into the deep descended,
  Cursed weed of China's coast;
Thus at once our fears were ended;
  British rights shall ne'er be lost.

Captains! once more hoist your streamers,
Spread your sails, and plough the wave;
Tell your masters they were dreamers,
When they thought to cheat the brave.

[1] *Ere the deathless deed be done.* During the operations of the savages, on board the tea-ships, a watch was stationed to prevent embezzlement, and not a single ounce of the commodity was suffered to be purloined by the populace. One or two persons being detected, in endeavoring to pocket a small quantity, were "stripped of their acquisitions and very roughly handled. Although a considerable quantity of merchandise, of different kinds, remained on board the vessels, no injury was sustained. Such attention to private property was observed, that a small padlock, belonging to the captain of one of the ships, being broke, another was procured and sent to him." *Freeman's Journal.*

A Lady's adieu to her tea-table, published a short time after the destruction of the tea at Boston.

Farewell the tea-board, with its gaudy equipage
Of cups and saucers, cream bucket, sugar tongs,
The pretty tea chest also, lately stored
With Hyson, Congo, and best double fine.
Full many a joyous moment I've sat by ye,
Hearing the girls tattle, the old maids talk scandal,
And the spruce coxcomb laugh at—may-be—nothing.
No more shall I dish out the once loved liquor,
Though now detestable,
Because I'm taught, and believe it true,
Its use will fasten slavish chains upon my country.
For Liberty's the goodess I would choose
To reign triumphant in America.

Virginia Banishing Tea.

1774.

Many urgent appeals to the people of the different colonies were made after the destruction of the tea at Boston, calling upon them to abstain from the use of all imported commodities, and to confine themselves to the fragrant herbs and other productions of their own fields and forests. The following poetical one was written by a young lady, of whom all that is known is, that she was " a native of Virginia, endowed with all the graces of a cultivated mind, pleasant external qualities, and a model of patriotism worthy the emulation of many more conspicuous."

VIRGINIA BANISHING TEA.

BEGONE, pernicious, baneful tea,
  With all Pandora's ills possessed,
Hyson, no more beguiled by thee[1]
  My noble sons shall be oppressed.

To Britain fly, where gold enslaves,
   And venal men their birth-right sell;
Tell *North* and his bribed clan of knaves,
   Their bloody acts were made in hell.

In Henry's reign those acts began,
   Which sacred rules of justice broke
North now pursues the hellish plan,
   To fix on us his slavish yoke.

But we oppose, and will be free,
   This great good cause we will defend;
Nor bribe, nor Gage, nor North's decree,
   Shall make us " at his feet to bend."

From Anglia's ancient sons we came;
   Those heroes who for freedom fought;
In freedom's cause we'll march; their fame,
   By their example greatly taught.

Our king we love, but North we hate,
   Nor will to him submission own;
If death's our doom, we'll brave our fate,
   But pay allegiance to the throne.

Then rouse, my sons ! from slavery free
Your suffering homes; from God's high wrath ;
Gird on your steel ; give *liberty*
To all who follow in our path.

[1] *Hyson, no more beguiled by thee.* These appeals, very generally, had the desired effects. Some, however, of the " more ancient and decaide females," could not deny themselves the pleasing stimulant, and it was their custom to take a "wee drop" clandestinely. The following is one, of many anecdotes concerning these quiet solacements. " A lady of Virginia, being in opulent circumstances, invited a party of her female acquaintances to pass an evening with her in a private room up stairs, where they were to regale themselves with a dish of the forbidden tea. But the husband of the lady, inferring, from the appearance of affairs, what was going on, quietly stole up stairs and slipped a piece of tobacco into the tea-kettle. The consequence was, the ladies all went home most terribly disturbed and uncertain ; while the old gentleman enjoyed himself, *patriotically*, at their expense."

The Blasted Herb.

1774.

This ballad first appeared in Fowle's Gazette, on the twenty-second of July, 1774, but soon after was adapted to a sacred air, and published in a broadside. It has been attributed to Meshech Weare, who was president of the State of New Hampshire in 1776. He was born in 1714, graduated at Harvard College in 1735, and passing through the highest offices of the State in which he lived, died at Hampton Falls, in the early part of 1786.

INDIA TEA.

ROUSE every generous thoughtful mind,
   The rising danger flee,
If you would lasting freedom find,
   Now then abandon tea.

Scorn to be bound with golden chains,
  Though they allure the sight;
Bid them defiance, if they claim.
  Our freedom and birth-right.

Shall we our freedom give away,
  And all our comfort place
In drinking of outlandish tea,
  Only to please our taste?

Forbid it Heaven, let us be wise,
  And seek our country's good;
Nor ever let a thought arise,
  That tea should be our food.

Since we so great a plenty have,
  Of all that's for our health;
Shall we that blasted herb receive,
  Impoverishing our wealth?

When we survey the breathless corpse,
  With putrid matter filled;
For crawling worms, a sweet resort,
  By us reputed ill.

Noxious effluvia sending out,
    From its pernicious store,
Not only from the foaming mouth,
    But every lifeless pore.

To view the same enrolled in tea,
    Besmeared with such perfumes,
And then the herb sent o'er the sea,
    To us it tainted comes—

Some of it tinctured with a filth,
    Of carcasses embalmed;
Taste of this herb, then, if thou wilt!
    Sure me it cannot charm.

Adieu! away, oh tea! begone!
    Salute our taste no more;
Though thou art coveted by some
    Who're destined to be poor.

Gage's Proclamation.

1774.

Thomas Hutchinson was recalled to England early in 1774, and General Gage appointed as his successor in the office of governor of Massachusetts Bay. On his arrival at Boston, in May of that year, Gage immediately issued a proclamation, calling upon the inhabitants to be loyal, and again return to the friendship of an injured sovereign, assuring them at the same time, that the royal authority would be supported at all hazards. This proclamation was versified in many parts of the colonies, and in various instances, published as a ballad. From among a great number we select the following, which first appeared in the Virginia Gazette, as a " friendly warning."

A PROCLAMATION.

AMERICA ! thou fractious nation,
Attend thy master's proclamation !
Tremble ! for know, I, Thomas Gage,[1]
Determin'd came the war to wage.

With the united powers sent forth,
Of Bute, of Mansfield, and of North;
To scourge your insolence, my choice,
While England mourns and Scots rejoice!

Bostonia first shall feel my power,
And gasping midst the dreadful shower
Of ministerial rage, shall cry,
Oh, save me, Bute! I yield! and die.

Then shall my thundering cannons rattle,
My hardy veterans march to battle,
Against Virginia's hostile land,
To humble that rebellious band.[2]

At my approach her trembling swains,
Shall quit well-cultivated plains,
To seek the inhospitable wood;
Or try, like swine of old, the flood.

Rejoice! ye happy Scots rejoice!
Your voice lift up, a mighty voice,
The voice of gladness on each tongue,
The mighty praise of Bute be sung.

The praise of Mansfield, and of North,
Let next your hymns of joy set forth,
Nor shall the rapturous strain assuage,
Till sung's your own proclaiming Gage.

Whistle ye pipes! ye drones drone on.
Ye bellows blow! Virginia's won!
Your Gage has won Virginia's shore,
And Scotia's sons shall mourn no more.

Hail Middlesex! oh happy county![3]
Thou too shalt share thy master's bounty,
Thy sons obedient, naught shall fear,
Thy wives and widows drop no tear.

Thrice happy people, ne'er shall feel
The force of unrelenting steel;
What brute would give the ox a stroke
Who bends his neck to meet the yoke?

To Murray bend the humble knee;[4]
He shall protect you under me;
His generous pen shall not be mute,
But sound your praise thro' Fox to Bute.

By Scotchmen lov'd, by Scotchmen taught,
By all your country Scotchmen thought;
Fear Bute, fear Mansfield, North and me,
And be as blest as slaves can be.

[1] *Tremble! for know I, Thomas Gage.* Thomas Gage was the last royal governor of Massachusetts. He was appointed governor of Montreal in 1760, and in 1763 was commissioned commander-in-chief of all the royal forces in North America. In the government of Massachusetts, he inflicted the people of Boston with the most rigorous laws and restrictions, thinking it a duty he owed his king, and his departure for England in the fall of 1775, was hailed, by those people, with unbounded joy. He died in 1787.

[2] *To humble that rebellious band.* The people of Virginia at all times resisted the attempts of Parliament to tax them without their consent. The bold declaration of Patrick Henry, before the House of Burgesses, in 1764, that " Cæsar had his Brutus—Charles the First his Cromwell ; and George the Third may profit by their example," still rang in the ears of royalty, and the patriots were looked upon as a " rebellious band that must be broken."

[3] *Hail Middlesex! oh happy county!* An inconsiderable number of the inhabitants of the county of Middlesex, in Virginia, during the early part of 1774, undertook to make some resolves, contradictory to the general sentiment of that colony. That gave occasion to the following production, written by a " Lady of Pennsylvania."

> To manhood he makes a vain pretence,
> Who wants both manly force and sense ;
> 'Tis but the form and not the matter,
> According to the schoolmen's clatter ;
> From such a creature, Heaven defend her!
> Each lady cries, no *neuter gender !*
> But when a number of such creatures,
> With woman's hearts and manly features,
> Their country's generous schemes perplex,
> I own I hate this Middle-sex.

⁴ *To Murray bend the humble knee.* John Murray, earl of Dunmore, was governor of Virginia from 1770 till 1775. In the month of April, 1775, he removed the royal stores and ammunition at Williamsburg, Virginia, on board some armed vessels, and afterwards abandoned his office and went into active service for the king. His depredations and cruelties, in the southern colonies, have become matters of history. Dunmore sailed for England in 1776, and never returned to America. He was shortly afterwards appointed governor of Bermuda, but did not remain there long, on account of his unpopularity. He died in England in 1809.

Maryland Resolves.

1 7 7 4.

About the middle of December, **1774**, deputies appointed by the freemen of the province of Maryland, met at Annapolis, unanimously resolved to resist the authority of Parliament, taxing the colonies, if attempted to be enforced, and to support the acts and designs of the Continental Congress at all hazards. They also recommended that every man should provide himself " a good firelock, with bayonet attached, powder and ball, and be in readiness to act in any emergency." These resolutions were productive of many ludicrous and bombastic ballads. From among these, the one following, adapted to the air "Abbot of Canterbury, or Wilkes' Wriggle," is selected.[1]

MARYLAND RESOLVES.

ON Calvert's plains new faction reigns,
   Great Britain we defy, sir,
True liberty lies gagg'd in chains,
   Though freedom is the cry, sir.

The Congress, and their factious tools,
  Most wantonly oppress us,
Hypocrisy triumphant rules,
  And sorely does distress us.

The British bands with glory crown'd,
  No longer shall withstand us ;
Our martial deeds loud fame shall sound
  Since mad Lee now commands us.[2]

Triumphant soon a blow he'll strike,
  That all the world shall awe, sir,
And General Gage, Sir Perseus like,
  Behind his wheels he'll draw, sir.

When Gallic hosts, ungrateful men,
  Our race meant to extermine,
Pray did committees save us then,
  Or Hancock, or such vermin ?

Then faction spurn ! think for yourselves !
  Your parent state, believe me,
From real griefs, from factious elves,
  Will speedily relieve ye.

[1] *Maryland resolves.* This song was published in Rivington's Gazette, with the accompanying letter, from its anonymous author, to the editor of that paper. " You, no doubt, have seen the resolves of certain magnates, naming themselves a Provincial Congress! I will not say these worthies are under the influence of the moon, or are proper subjects for confinement, but one of their resolves is exactly calculated for the meridian of the inquisition, and the others smell furiously of Bedlam. I gladly contribute my humble mite to ridicule the folly, ingratitude, and violence of our deluded patriots."

[2] *Since mad Lee now commands us.* Major-general Charles Lee, was an officer in the British Army, at the age of eleven years. He served under Abercrombie, at the unsuccessful attack of Ticonderoga, and was wounded. Under General Burgoyne, in Portugal, he distinguished himself. After this, he spent a few years in rambling over Europe, and some time in the Polish service, finally sailing for New York, where he arrived just in time to embrace the cause of the Colonists, which was now grown serious and decided. He received a commission from the Continental Congress in 1775, and was very active during the war, until the battle of Monmouth, where he disobeyed the orders of the commander-in-chief, and, by this means, threw the troops into confusion. He was reprimanded by Washington, and in the warmth of his resentment used improper language in return. For this he was tried by court martial, found guilty, and suspended from duty for twelve months. He made a splendid defence of his course, but Congress confirmed the sentence, which was like a mortal wound to his ambitious spirit. When he heard the confirmation he exclaimed, pointing to his dog, " *Oh that I were that animal that I might not call man my brother.*" He became vindictive, and abused General Washingt n in his conversation and writings. Finding himself abandoned by his friends, he retired to his plantation, in Virginia, where he amused himself with his books and dogs, and in the autumn of 1782, weary of his life, he went to Philadelphia, where he died soon after, calling upon his " *brave grenadiers to stand by him.*"

In his will, he earnestly desired that he might not be buried in any churchyard, or within one mile of a Presbyterian or Anabaptist meeting-house, as he "had kept so much bad company when alive, he did not choose to continue it when dead."

Lee's character is very correctly portrayed, in a letter from Mrs. Mercy Warren to Samuel Adams, where she speaks of him as "plain in his person to a degree of ugliness; careless even to unpoliteness; his garb ordinary; his voice rough; his manners rather morose; yet sensible, learned, judicious and penetrating."

The celebrated Thomas Paine once said, that Lee "*was above all monarchs and below all scum.*" *Thacher's Journal.*

Loyal York.

1775.

In January, 1775, William Franklin, the governor of the colony of New Jersey, addressed the legislature, warning them not to sanction certain proceedings connected with the dispute existing between the mother country and the colonies, assuring them, that all their grievances would be redressed on petition. Lieutenant-governor Colden, of New York, followed in the same path, and had great success with the New York Assembly; the majority of that body agreeing not to send delegates to the Congress, that was to assemble in May of that year. This success was a triumph for the loyalists, and was the cause of great rejoicing. The following song of exultation appeared a short time after the event, in the Gazetteer, at New York, and has been attributed to Rivington, the editor of that paper; but without any authority.

LOYAL YORK.

AND so, my good master, I find 'tis no joke,
For York has stepp'd forward, and thrown off the yoke
Of Congress, committees, and even King Sears,[1]
Who shows you good nature, by showing his ears.

I trembled lest York should have join'd the mad freak,
And formèd a part of the damnable sneak;
The fever abated, see order arise,
With ag'd constitutional tears in her eyes.

Having summon'd her sons, who too wantonly stray'd,
And calling her fair sister Grace to her aid,
The youth she address'd, in such accents of love,
As coming from mothers, ought always to move.

Says she, " My dear children, ah ! why should ye roam,
In quest of rude discord, and leave me at home ?
Your godfather Monarchy, bleeds at the heart,
To think that his sons should from virtue depart.

" Consider how long we have cherish'd, protected,
How much we've indulg'd, and how little corrected,
How oft we're provok'd, and our councils tormented;
What insults forgiven, what bloodshed prevented.

" Behold your good brother, who rules in the north,
Examine his conduct and copy his worth :
Observe how Apollo presides, and you'll find,
How lovely are mercy and power combin'd.

" His task, though severe, he discharges with ease,
And studies, like us, to preserve and to please ;
Oh ! think how he feels, between brother and brother,
When he's sent to reconcile one to the other.

" Then cease, I beseech you, nor longer provoke
The hand, which so tenderly wards off the stroke.
Such counsel as this was enough, one would think,
To save them from ruin, though just on the brink.

" But would you believe, a committee they'd choose,
Consisting of three, who had nothing to lose ?
One was a cock of the first game,
Who hand over hand was determin'd on fame.

" The second A-dam dog who lives upon strife,
And knows nought but hemp can lead him a worse life :
The third was a Cooper,[2] good Lord, long preserve him,
Or, as I want rhyme, may his customers starve him !

" Together they went on a grand consultation,
To prove a republic was good for the nation,
And to show the old dame, it was easily prov'd,
Pronounced, by four words, all objections remov'd.

" Inestimable rights, infernal chains,"
A sleeping potion for a Briton's brains.—
The aged matron silently withdrew,
Wept for her sons, and left them, Gage ! to you.

[1] *King Sears.* "Isaac Sears was born at Norwalk, Connecticut, in 1729. He was a successful merchant in the city of New York, when political matters attracted his attention. When the Stamp Act aroused the colonists, Sears stood forth as the champion of right, and was one of the most active and zealous members of the association of the Sons of Liberty." He was celebrated during the war for his self-denial, and devotion to the cause of liberty. He died at Canton, where he had gone with a cargo, in 1785. *Lossing's Field Book.*

[2] *The third was a Cooper.* Dr. Cooper, town clerk of Boston, called by Rivington, " the fragrant Rose of Sharon."

Banks of the Dee.

1775.

This beautiful song was very popular, both in England and the colonies. It was composed by John Tait, a writer to the Signet, and, for some time, a judge in one of the minor courts at Edinburgh. It is adapted to the Irish air called *Langolee*. The song has often, though erroneously, been attributed to the Rev. John Home, author of the tragedy of " Douglass." It was first printed in the Pennsylvania Ledger, at Philadelphia, and also inserted in Wilson's collection, published at Edinburgh in 1779, with some additional stanzas, written by a lady; but her verses are far inferior to the original.

BANKS OF THE DEE.[1]

'Twas summer, and softly the breezes were blowing,
And sweetly the nightingale sang from the tree.
At the foot of a hill, where the river was flowing,
I sat myself down on the banks of the Dee.[2]

Flow on, lovely Dee, flow on thou sweet river,
Thy banks, purest stream, shall be dear to me ever,
For there I first gain'd the affection and favor
Of Jamie, the glory and pride of the Dee.

But now he's gone from me, and left me thus mourning,
To quell the proud rebels, for valiant is he ;
But ah ! there's no hope of his speedy returning,
To wander again on the banks of the Dee :
He's gone, hapless youth, o'er the rude roaring billows,
The kindest, the sweetest, of all his brave fellows ;
And left me to stray 'mongst these once lovèd willows,
The loneliest lass on the banks of the Dee.

But time and my prayers may perhaps yet restore him,
Blest peace may restore my dear lover to me,
And when he returns, with such care I'll watch o'er him,
He never shall leave the sweet banks of the Dee.
The Dee then will flow, all its beauty displaying,
The lambs on its banks will again be seen playing,
Whilst I, with my Jamie, am carelessly straying,
And tasting again all the sweets of the Dee.

[1] *The banks of the Dee* was written in 1775, on the departure of
a friend for America, to join the British forces, who were, at that

time, endeavoring "to quell the proud rebels" of Columbia ; but the issue of that contest was very different from the anticipations of the bard.

[2] *The banks of the Dee.* Robert Burns, in a letter to George Thomson, dated 7th April, 1793, says, " *The banks of the Dee,* is, you know, literally *Langolee,* to slow time. The song is well enough, but has some false imagery in it, for instance,

> 'And sweetly the nightingale sang from the tree.'

" In the first place, the nightingale sings in a low bush, but never from a tree ; and in the second place, there never was a nightingale seen or heard on the banks of the Dee, or on the banks of any other river in Scotland. Exotic rural imagery is always comparatively flat."

The justice of these remarks seems to have been allowed by Mr. Tait ; for in a new edition of the song, retouched by himself, some years after, for Mr. Thomson's collection, the first half stanza is printed thus :—

> " 'Twas summer, and softly the breezes were blowing,
> And sweetly the wood pigeon coo'd from the tree.
> At the foot of a rock, where the wild rose was growing,
> I sat myself down on the banks of the Dee."
>
> *Shenstone's Lyrics.*

A Parody.

1775.

This excellent parody is attributed to Oliver Arnold,[1] a native of Norwich, Connecticut, and a kinsman of the traitor. He wrote much doggerel during his time, some of which is quite good, and was, at the time, very popular.

BANKS OF THE DEE.

Twas winter, and blue tory noses were freezing,
As they march'd o'er the land where they ought not to be;
The valiants complain'd at the fifers' curs'd wheezing,
And wish'd they'd remain'd on the banks of the Dee.
Lead on thou paid captain! tramp on thou proud minions!
Thy ranks, basest men, shall be strung like ripe onions,
For here thou hast found heads with warlike opinions,
On the shoulders of nobles who ne'er saw the Dee.

Prepare for war's conflict; or make preparation
For peace with the rebels, for they're brave and glee;
Keep mindful of dying, and leave the foul nation
That sends out its armies to brag and to flee.
Make haste, now, and leave us thou miscreant tories!
To Scotland repair! there court the sad houris,
And listen once more to their plaints and their stories
Concerning the "glory and pride of the Dee."

Be quiet and sober, secure and contented:
Upon your own land, be valiant and free;
Bless God, that the war is so nicely prevented,
And till the green fields on the banks of the Dee.
The Dee then will flow, all its beauty displaying,
The lads on its banks will again be seen playing,
And England thus honestly taxes defraying,
With natural drafts from the banks of the Dee.

---

[1] *Oliver Arnold*, was celebrated for his ready wit at repartee. At the time Joel Barlow, (who was on terms of intimacy with him,) was enjoying much notoriety, for his revised and altered edition of Watts's Psalms and Hymns, Arnold presented him with the following stanzas:

> "You've proved yourself a sinful cre'tur;
> You've murder'd Watts and spoil'd the metre;
> You've tried the word of God to alter,
> And for your pains deserve a halter."

Liberty's Call.

1775.

The authorship of this chaste ballad has been assigned to one Jere. Sargent, of Philadelphia, a person of whom little is known; and also to Francis Hopkinson, the author of "The Battle of the Kegs." But, it is most probable, that it was written by the "eccentric John Mason,"[1] an operative in the office of the Pennsylvania Packet, the newspaper in which it first appeared. The late Mr. Hunnewell, of Watertown, Massachusetts, well remembered its popularity, and attributed it to Mason.

LIBERTY'S CALL.

HIGH on the banks of Delaware,
    Fair Liberty she stood;
And waving with her lovely hand,
    Cried, " Still, thou roaring flood.

Be still ye winds, be still ye seas,
   Let only zephyrs play!"
Just as she spoke, they all obeyed;
   And thus the maid did say:

" Welcome my friends, from every land
   Where freedom doth not reign;
Oh! hither fly from every clime,
   Sweet liberty to gain.

" Mark Londonderry's brave defence
   'Gainst tyranny that swayed;
Americans, the example's great!
   Like them, be not dismayed.

" Expect not that on downy beds,
   This boon you can secure;
At perils smile, rouse up your souls'
   War's dangers to endure.

" 'Gainst your affronted land behold
   Oppression rear its head;
In hydra-form and battle's din,
   Each trembling slave to dread.

" But ye, its sons, will ne'er give up
 Your parent fires till death ;
Behold ! yon beauteous virgins seek
 Laurel your brows to wreathe.

" Bear on your minds the noble deeds
 Your ancestors achieved ;
How many worthy Britons bled,
 To have their children freed !

" See on the meteors of the night
 Their spirits wanly fly !
Roused from their graves by your distress ;
 Hark ! thus I heard them cry.

" ' Was it for this, ye mothers dear !
 Ye nursed your tender babes ?
Was it for this, our yet loved sons !
 We sheathed our trusty blades ?

" ' O ! genius of our ancient times !
 Be thou our children's guide,
To arms ! to arms ! '—They call to arms,
 And stalk in martial pride.

" I will them guide, ye reverend sires !
        Go to your tombs in peace ;
    The rage of proud usurping men,
        Your sons shall yet repress.

" Hold up your heads, ye weeping fair !
        Their swords are on their thighs ;
    Smile yet again, ye lovely babes !
        Their banner's in the skies.

" I come, I come, to join your train ;
        Heaven's ministers I see ;
    Farewell, my friends, be not afraid !
        Be virtuous and be free ! "

    Heaven's portals opened as she soared,
        And angels thence did come ;
    With heavenly songs and golden harps,
        The Goddess welcomed home.

---

[1] *Eccentric John Mason.* This gentleman was a native of Maryland. In early life he went to Philadelphia, where little was known
of him, until he commenced work at the office of Dunlap's Pennsylvania Packet, a paper strenuously devoted to the cause of liberty.
During the earlier part of the Revolution, Mason was accustomed,
privately, to print and circulate squibs, pasquinades and epigrams,

bearing severely on the royal cause, and in a measure gained the hatred of many friends of the crown, whom he often made the subject of his ridicule. He combined the trade of a printer with that of an upholsterer, and kept a shop in Arch street, Philadelphia, opposite the gate of the Friends' burying-ground, where he carried on "Upholstery in all its various branches," besides making his shop a depot for the circulation of his "little billets of ridicule." On the approach of the British, in 1777, Mason removed his store from the city, and abandoned for ever the "setting of types." About one year after, the following advertisement appeared in his old friend, the Pennsylvania Packet:

"JOHN MASON, UPHOLDER.

"Carries on the Upholdstery business in all its various branches, and shall be extremely obliged to those noble and generous ladies and gentlemen who delight in employing the industrious.

"Said Mason begs leave to inform his former friends and customers, that when the enemy marched into this city, he, the said Mason, marched out, and since that time has had many a march and counter-march, and now has had the happiness to march back again to a city where slavery could not thrive, because there liberty springs spontaneous.

> "Ah! slavery, how loved, how valued
> Once, avails thee not; to whom
> Related or by whom begot;
> A painful nuisance alone
> Remains of thee.——
> 'Tis all thou art, and it is all
> Thy proud friends and abettors shall be."

Alphabet

FOR LITTLE MASTERS AND MISSES.

1775.

This production appeared in a ballad sheet in the early part of 1775, and was afterwards reprinted in the Constitutional Gazette, with a slight abridgment in the text.

ALPHABET.

A, stands for Americans, who scorn to be slaves;

B, for Boston, where fortitude their freedom saves;

C, stands for Congress, which, though loyal, will be free;

D, stands for defence, 'gainst force and tyranny.

> Stand firmly, A and Z,
>
> We swear for ever to be free!

E, stands for evils, which a civil war must bring;

F, stands for fate, dreadful to both people and king;

G, stands for George, may God give him wisdom and grace;

H, stands for hypocrite, who wears a double face.

J, stands for justice, which traitors in power defy,
K, stands for king, who should to such the axe apply;
L, stands for London, to its country ever true,
M, stands for Mansfield, who hath another view.

N, stands for North, who to the House the mandate brings,
O, stands for oaths, binding on subjects not on kings:
P, stands for people, who their freedom should defend,
Q, stands for *quere*, when will England's troubles end?

R, stands for rebels, not at Boston but at home,
S, stands for Stuart, sent by Whigs abroad to roam,
T, stands for Tories, who may try to bring them back,
V, stands for villains, who have well deserved the rack.

W, stands for Wilkes, who us from warrants saved,
Y, for York, the New, half corrupted, half enslaved,
Z, stands for Zero, but means the Tory minions,
Who threatens us with fire and sword, to bias our opinions.

Stand firmly A and Z,
We swear for ever to be free!

The Pennsylvania Song.

1 7 7 5.

The author of this ballad is unknown. It appeared originally in the "Poet's Corner" of Dunlap's Packet, as the "Pennsylvania March, to the tune of the Scots' song, "*I winna marry ony lad, but Sandy o'er the lea.*"

PENNSYLVANIA SONG.

WE are the troop that ne'er will stoop
    To wretched slavery,
Nor shall our seed, by our base deed
    Despisèd vassals be ;
Freedom we will bequeathe to them,
    Or we will bravely die ;
Our greatest foe, ere long shall know,
    How much did Sandwich lie.
        And all the world shall know,
           Americans are free ;
        Nor slaves nor cowards we will prove,
           Great Britain soon shall see.

We'll not give up our birthright,
    Our foes shall find us men ;
As good as they, in any shape,
    The British troops shall kèn.
Huzza ! brave boys, we'll beat them
    On any hostile plain ;
For freedom, wives, and children dear,
    The battle we'll maintain.

What ! can those British tyrants think,
    Our fathers cross'd the main,
And savage foes, and dangers met,
    To be enslav'd by them ?
If so, they are mistaken,
    For we will rather die ;
And since they have become our foes,
    Their forces we defy.
        And all the world shall know,
           Americans are free,
        Nor slaves nor cowards we will prove,
           Great Britain soon shall see.

The Irishman's Epistle.

1775.

This happy production of "Paddy," must have been very popular with "the rebels," as there were four different editions of it published as broadsides, a short time after its first appearance, in the Pennsylvania Magazine. The version subjoined, was printed in May, 1775, and differs slightly in language from that contained in the periodical.

THE EPISTLE TO THE TROOPS IN BOSTON.

By my faith, but I think ye're all makers of bulls,
With your brains in your breeches, your —— in your
    skulls,
Get home, with your muskets, and put up your swords,
And look in your books for the meaning of words.
You see now, my honies, how much your mistaken,
For Concord by discord¹ can never be beaten.

How brave ye went out with your muskets all bright,
And thought to be-frighten the folks with the sight;
But when you got there how they powder'd your pums,
And all the way home how they pepper'd your ——,
And is it not, honeys, a comical crack,
To be proud in the face, and be shot in the back.

How come ye to think, now, they did not know how,[2]
To be after their firelocks as smartly as you?
Why, you see now, my honies, 'tis nothing at all,
But to pull at the trigger, and pop goes the ball.

And what have you got now with all your designing,
But a town without victuals to sit down and dine in;
And to look on the ground like a parcel of noodles,
And sing, how the Yankees have beaten the Doodles.
I'm sure if you're wise you'll make peace for a dinner,
For fighting and fasting will soon make ye thinner.

[1] "*For Concord by discord*," &c. Puns upon the word Concord
were numberless, after the action of the nineteenth of April, 1775.
The following appeared as " an anecdote," shortly after that action.
" When the emigrants and adventurers first came to America, they
met on the shore with Calvinists, Huguenots, Papists and Protestants.
Such a medley of people, of different tenets and persuasions, promised much discord ; however, good sense prevailed, and they unan-

imously agreed that no difference in opinion should disturb the public tranquillity, but that they would live in all brotherly love with
each other, and they named the first founded spot, and town, *Concord.* Is it not whimsical, that upon this spot they should first
draw blood, and gallantly contend for the rights and liberties of
America?

  [2] *They did not know how.* The following brief account of the affairs at Lexington and Concord, is taken from a letter dated Boston,
April 19, 1775. " Last night, at about eleven o'clock, one thousand
of the best troops, in a very secret manner, rowed up the Cambridge
River, and landed.   From whence they marched to Lexington,
where they saw a number of men exercising. They ordered them
to disperse, and immediately fired on them; killed eight men on
the spot, and then marched to Concord. This alarmed the country
so, that it seemed as if men came down from the clouds. This news
coming to town, General Gage sent out another thousand men, with
a large train of artillery. In the mean time, those troops at Concord had set fire to the court-house. There an engagement ensued,
and the King's troops retreated very fast, until they were reinforced
with the troops the General had sent: but they did not stand long
before the whole body gave way; retreating, and our men keeping
up at their heels, loading and firing, until they got to Charlestown,
when our people thought it not prudent to come any further, fearing
the ships in the harbor would be ordered to fire on Boston and
Charlestown. Our men behaved gallantly." One poor fellow, who
had received a wound in his breast, in following up the retreat, was
offered assistance by a brother soldier, when he remarked, " I am
beyond your assistance — pursue the enemy ! " — and with these
words on his lips, fell back and died.—*Virginia Gazette.*

Breed's Hill.

1 7 7 5.

During the battle, upon this hill, the village of Charlestown was destroyed. The subjoined lyric, commemorating the event, has been attributed to Joel Barlow. He composed various patriotic songs, many of which are familiar. On entering the army, he wrote, " I do not know, whether I shall do more for the cause in the capacity of chaplain, than I could in that of poet ; I have great faith in the influence of songs ; and shall continue, while fulfilling the duties of my appointment, to write one now and then, and to encourage the taste for them which I find in the camp. One good song is worth a dozen addresses or proclamations." [1]

THE BURNING OF CHARLESTOWN.

PALMYRA'S prospect, with her tumbling walls,
   Huge piles of ruin heap'd on every side,
From each beholder, tears of pity calls,
   Sad monuments, extending far and wide.

Yet far more dismal to the patriot's eye,
　The drear remains of Charlestown's former show,
Behind whose walls did hundred warriors die,
　And Britain's centre felt the fatal blow.

To see a town so elegantly form'd,
　Such buildings graced with every curious art,
Spoil'd in a moment, on a sudden storm'd,
　Must fill with indignation every heart.

But when we find the reasons of her fate
　To be but trifling — trifling did I say ?
For being noble! daring to be great,
　Nor calmly yielding to tyrannic sway !

To see the relics of that once famed place,
　Pointing to Heaven, as 'twere in ardent cry,
By lawless power robb'd of every grace,
　Yet calling bolts of vengeance from on high :

To find, I say, such dealings with mankind,
　To see those royal robbers planted near
Those glorious buildings, turning into wind,
　And loath to mingle with the common air.

And such chastisement coming from a state
   Who calls herself our parent, nurse, and friend—
Must rouse each soul that's noble, frank, and great,
   And urge us on our lives and all to spend!

Oh! spot once graceful; but, alas! no more;
   Till signs shall end, and time itself shall cease,
Thy name shall live, and on fame's pinions soar,
   To mark grim blackness on Great Britain's face.

Nor shall the blood of heroes on the plain,
   Who nobly fell that day in freedom's cause,
Lie unreveng'd, though with thy thousands slain,[2]
   Whilst there's a King who fears nor minds thy laws.

Shall Cain who madly spilt his brother's blood,
   Receive such curses from the God of all?
Is not that Sovereign still as just and good,
   To hear the cries of children when they call?

Yes, there's a God whose laws are still the same,
   Whose years are endless, and his power is great;
He is our God : Jehovah is his name;
   With him we trust our sore oppressèd state.

5

When he shall rise (oh, Britain, dread the day,
  Nor can I stretch the period of thy fate);
What heart of steel, what tyrant then shall sway,
  A throne that's sinking by oppression's weight?

Thy crimes, oh North, shall then like spectres stand,
  Nor Charlestown hindmost in the ghastly roll,
And faithless Gage, who gave the dread command,
  Shall find dire torments gnaw upon his soul.

Yea, in this world, we trust that ills so dread,
  Which fills the nation with such matchless woes,
Shall fall with double vengeance on thy head,
  Nor 'scape those minions which thy court compose.

[1] Curiosities of American Literature, by Rufus W. Griswold.

[2] *Thy thousands slain.* Shortly after the battle of Breed's Hill, the following epigram appeared on a large handbill:

> " *The modern veni, vidi, vici.*
>
> We came, we saw, but could not beat,
> And so—we sounded a retreat;
> On Roxbury Hill again we saw 'em,
> And did, like devils, clapper-claw 'em;
> But warlike casuists can't discuss,
> If we beat them, or they beat us;
> We swear we beat, they swear we lie,
> We'll tell you more on't bye and bye."

𝕬𝕯𝖆𝖒'𝖘 𝕱𝖆𝖑𝖑:

THE TRIP TO CAMBRIDGE.

1775.

Notwithstanding the prominent position in which General Washington was placed at the head of an undisciplined army, and the effect which that position produced upon the minds of the well regulated and disdainful royal troops, he was the subject of a very few ludicrous ballads. The ministerial writers generally burlesqued the great common interests of the people, in their productions, or comprehended the whole race of patriots as one *rebel* collection.

TRIP TO CAMBRIDGE.

WHEN Congress sent great Washington [1]
All clothed in power and breeches,
To meet old Britain's warlike sons
And make some rebel speeches;

'Twas then he took his gloomy way [2]
   Astride his dapple donkeys,
And travelled well, both night and day,
   Until he reach'd the Yankees

Away from camp, 'bout three miles off,
   From Lily he dismounted, [3]
His sergeant brush'd his sun-burnt wig
   While he the specie counted.

All prinked up in *full* bag-wig;
   The shaking notwithstanding,
In leathers tight, oh ! glorious sight !
   He reach'd the Yankee landing. [4]

The women ran, the darkeys too ;
   And all the bells, they tollèd ;
For Britain's sons, by Doodle doo,
   We're sure to be—consolèd.

Old mother Hancock with a pan
   All crowded full of butter,
Unto the lovely Georgius ran,
   And added to the splutter.

Says she, " Our brindle has just calved,
    And John is wondrous happy.
He sent this present to you, dear,
    As you're the ' country's papa.' "—

" You'll butter bread and bread butter,
    But do not butt your speeches.
" You'll butter bread and bread butter,
    But do not grease your breeches."

Full many a child went into camp,
    All dressed in homespun kersey,
To see the greatest rebel scamp
    That ever cross'd o'er Jersey.

The rebel clowns, oh ! what a sight !
    Too awkward was their figure.
'Twas yonder stood a pious wight,
    And here and there a nigger.

Upon a stump, he placed (himself,)
    Great Washington did he,
And through the nose of lawyer Close [5]
    Proclaimed great Liberty. [6]

The patriot brave, the patriot fair,
From fervor had grown thinner,
So off they march'd, with patriot zeal,
And took a patriot dinner.[7]

[1] *When Congress sent great Washington.* Washington was appointed by the Continental Congress, " General and Commander-in-chief of all the troops raised and to be raised, for the defence of the United Colonies," in June 1775, and immediately set off to join the main army, which was at Cambridge, Massachusetts.

[2] *'Twas then he took his gloomy way.* On the journey he was treated with the highest honors in every place through which he passed. Volunteers of gentlemen and ladies often escorting him through their villages.

[3] *From Lily he dismounted.* "The delicate name of this donkey was probably suggested to Washington by the whiteness of its hide, which was pretty well exposed to the weather, from the constant chafing of the articles with which it was ladened, and by mange, which through the mysterious operations of nature, and bad care, will appear on the outer wall of the animal kingdom."

Author of the Song.

[4] *He reach'd the Yankee landing.* He arrived at Cambridge on the 3d of July, where he was received with every mark of respect by the people, and the joyful acclamations of the soldiers.

[5] *Lawyer Close.* This must refer to the general's aid, Major Lee.

[6] *Proclaimed great Liberty.* At the head of his army, he issued a proclamation, of which the following is part : " In our own native land, in defence of the freedom which is our birthright, and which we ever enjoyed till the late violation of it, we have taken up arms; we shall lay them down when hostilities shall cease on the part of the aggressors, and all danger of their being renewed, shall be removed ; and not before."

[7] *A patriot dinner.* "Corn pudding and Yankee rum, a great promoter of rebellion and riot." *Author of the Song.*

A New Song.

1775.

J. W. Hewlings, the author of this ballad "on the present critical times," was a native of Nansemond, Virginia, where he died, in the early part of the year 1793.

AMERICAN "HEARTS OF OAK."

Come rouse up my lads, and join this great cause,
In defence of your liberty, your property, and laws!
'Tis to honor we call you, stand up for your right,
And ne'er let our foes say, we are put to the flight.

>   For so just is our cause, and so valiant our men,
>   We always are ready, steady boys, steady;
>   We'll fight for our freedom again and again

The Scotch politicians have laid a deep scheme,
By invading America to bring Charlie in;
And if the Scotch mist's not remov'd from the throne,
The crown's not worth wearing, the kingdom's undone.

The placemen, and commoners, have taken a bribe
To betray their own country, and the empire beside;
And though the colonies stand condemned by some,
There are no rebels here, but are traitors at home.

The arbitrary minister, he acts as he please,
He wounds our constitution, and breaks through our laws;
His troops they are landed, his ships they are moor'd,
But boys all stand together, they will fall by the sword.

The great Magna Charta is wounded severe;
By accounts from the doctors, 'tis almost past cure.
Let's defend it with the sword, or die with the braves,
For we had better die in freedom, than live and be slaves.

They tax us contrary to reason and right,
Expecting that we are not able to fight;
But to draw their troop home, I do think would be best,
For Providence always defends the oppress'd.

The valiant Bostonians have enter'd the field,
And declare they will fall there before they will **yield**;
A noble example ! In them we'll confide,
We'll march to their town, stand or fall by their **side.**

An union through the colonies will ever **remain,**
And ministerial taxation will be but in **vain,**
For we are all resolvèd to die or be free ;
So they may repeal the acts, for repeal'd they **must be.**

Fish and Tea.

1775.

A NEW SONG TO AN OLD TUNE.

WHAT a court, hath old England, of folly and sin,
Spite of Chatham and Camden, Barre, Burke, Wilkes
    and Glynn!
Not content with the game act, they tax fish and sea,
And America drench with hot water and tea.
       Derry down, down, hey derry down.

Lord Sandwich, he swears they are terrible cowards,
Who can't be made brave by the blood of the Howards;
And to prove there is truth in America's fears,
He conjures Sir Peter's ghost 'fore the peers.

Now, indeed, if these poor people's nerves are so weak,
How cruel it is their destruction to seek!
Dr. Johnson's a proof, in the highest degree,
His soul and his system were changèd by tea.

But if the wise council of England doth think,
They may be enslaved by the power of drink,
They're right to enforce it; but then, do you see?
The Colonies, too, may refuse and be free.

There's no knowing where this oppression will stop;
Some say—there's no cure but a capital chop;
And that I believe's each American's wish,
Since you've drench'd them with tea, and depriv'd 'em
  of fish.

The birds of the air, and the fish of the sea,
By the gods, for poor Dan Adam's use were made free,
Till a man with more power, than old Moses would wish,
Said, " Ye wretches, ye shan't touch a fowl or a fish! "

Three Generals[1] these mandates have borne 'cross the sea,
To deprive 'em of fish and to make 'em drink tea;
In turn, sure, these freemen will boldly agree,
To give 'em a dance upon Liberty Tree.

Then *freedom's* the word, both at home and abroad,

And —— every scabbard that hides a good sword!

Our forefathers gave us this freedom in hand,

And we'll die in defence of the rights of the land.

     Derry down, down, hey derry down.

[1] *Three Generals.* The subjoined impromptu was published at London, by some friend of the colonies, on the departure of the British Generals for America:

> " Behold! the Cerberus the Atlantic plough,
> Her precious cargo, Burgoyne, Clinton, Howe—
> Bow! wow! wow!"

The Times.

1776.

Very many songs, bearing this title, were produced during the revolution. This spirited one was originally published as a broadside, early in 1776. At a later period, it appeared in a music-sheet, adapted to the "Tune of the sweeper: — Though I sweep to and fro."

THE TIMES.[1]

My muse now thy aid and assistance we claim,
Whilst freedom, dear freedom, affords us a theme,
Invok'd, be propitious, nor madly forbear,
When a theme that's so sacred should ring far and near.
  Oh! let freedom, and friendship, for ever remain,
    Nor that rascal draw breath, who would forge us a chain.

As our fathers have fought, and our grandfathers bled,
And many a hero now sleeps with the dead ;
Let us nobly defend, what they bravely maintain'd,
Nor suffer our sons to be fetter'd and chain'd.

The lion, the wolf, and the tiger may prey,
Each beast of the forest, though worse still than they.
May be brought as examples, yet where can we find
One so cruel, as sporting to kill their own kind.

Yet Briton's beware of the curse you maintain,
Your sons and your offspring we all still remain ;
Behold the most savage, and there you may see,
Their offspring more tenderly treated than we.

Though our foes may look on, and our friends **may**
admire,
How a BUTE or a NORTH, should set nations on fire,
Yet Satan, when suffer'd his madness to vent,
In meanest of mansions sure pitches his tent.

Shall freedom, that blessing sent down from above,
A manifest mark of God's wonderful love,
Be left at his will, who delights to annoy,
Whose pleasure is nought but to kill and destroy ?

Forbid it, ye gods, who preside o'er the land!
Forbid it, ye genii, who rule with the wand!
Forbid it, ye heroes, whoever draws breath!
Nor dread, in the combat, to rush upon death.

May our King be as wise as we mortals expect;
Each rascal from council then boldly eject;
May his life be as good, and his reign be as great,
As ever was Solomon's wonderful state.

Then curs'd be the foes of our birthright so dear,
May they never find comfort or happiness here!
But vagabond-like, o'er the earth may they stray,
Unshelter'd by night, and unfed through the day.

Let singular blessings America crown;
May the Congress be blest with immortal renown;
Each colony live in true sisterly peace,
Whilst harmony, honor, and riches increase.
    Oh! let freedom and friendship for ever remain,
    Nor that rascal draw breath, who would forge us a chain.

---

[1] *The Times.* In a version of this song, published in 1777, the
following couplet is added:

> "The times, it seems, are altered quite,
> The scales are cracked, the sword is broke,
> Right is now wrong, and wrong is right,
> And justice is a standing joke."

A New Song.

1776.

Though this song has but slight pretensions to literary merit, its subject long made it popular among the colonists. It was first printed in the Pennsylvania Magazine, and occasionally reprinted in the newspapers, as the war progressed. The melody to which it was adapted, "As Jamie gay blithe gang'd his way," probably increased its popularity.

COLLINET AND PHEBE.

As Collinet and Phebe sat,
　　Beneath a poplar grove,
The gentle youth, with fondest truth,
　　Was telling tales of love.

Dear blooming maid, the shepherd said,
  My tender vows believe,
These downcast eyes, and artless sighs,
  Can ne'er thy faith deceive.

Though some there are, from fair to fair,
  Delighting wild to rove,
Such change, thou ne'er, from me canst fear,
  Thy charms secure my love.

Then Phebe now, approve my vow,
  By truth, by fondness press'd;
A smile assume to grace thy bloom,
  And make thy shepherd bless'd.

A blush o'erspread her cheek with red,
  Which half she turn'd aside ;
With pleasing woes, her bosom rose,
  And thus the maid replied —

Dear gentle youth, I know thy truth,
  And all thy arts to please ;
But ah ! is this a time for bliss,
  Or themes as soft as these ?

While all around, we hear no sound,
  But war's terrific strains !
The drum commands our arming bands,
  And chides each tardy swain.

Our country's call, arouses all,
  Who dare be brave and free !
My love shall crown the youth alone,
  Who saves himself and me.

'Tis done ! he cried, from thy dear side,
  Now quickly I'll be gone ;
From love will I, to freedom fly,
  A slave to thee alone.

And when I come with laurels home,
  And all that freemen crave,
To crown my love, your smiles shall prove,
  The fair reward the brave.

[1] *The fair reward the brave.* On the departure of the able-bodied men " in the service of their country, the patriotic young women, to prevent the evil that would follow the neglect of putting in the crop, joined the ploughs and prepared the fallows for the seed ; and now, their fathers, brothers, and lovers, being detained, in the support of the liberties of these States, have determined to plant the seed themselves."—*Freeman's Journal,* 1776.

War Song.

1776.

It is supposed this song was first published in 1776. We have a music sheet containing it, and the "Liberty Song," bearing the following impress: "Portsmouth; printed by Benjamin Dearborn,[1] near the parade, 1776."

WAR SONG.

HARK, hark, the sound of war is heard,
 And we must all attend;
Take up our arms and go with speed,
 Our country to defend.

Our parent state has turned our foe,
 Which fills our land with pain;
Her gallant ships, manned out for war,
 Come thundering o'er the main.

There's Carleton, Howe, and Clinton too.
    And many thousands more,
May cross the sea, but all in vain,
    Our rights we'll ne'er give o'er.

Our pleasant homes they do invade,
    Our property devour ;
And all because we won't submit
    To their despotic power.

Then let us go against our foe,
    We'd better die than yield ;
We and our sons are all undone,
    If Britain wins the field.

Tories may dream of future joys,
    But I am bold to say,
They'll find themselves bound fast in chains,
    If Britain wins the day.

Husbands must leave their loving wives,
    And sprightly youths attend,
Leave their sweethearts and risk their lives,
    Their country to defend.

May they be heroes in the field,
Have heroes' fame in store;
We pray the Lord to be their shield,
Where thundering cannons roar.

[1] *Benjamin Dearborn* was the printer of the " Freeman's Journal, or New Hampshire Gazette," in which many fine songs were published. This one has been attributed to Dearborn, but we have no authority for saying that he ever wrote any other verse than the following, " which was posted on the front of his printing house."

The Printer has for sale within,
Kettles and cups, all formed of tin:
To such as want a service-cup,
Just open the door and hasten up!

Pennsylvania Packet.

A Song.

1776.

This song appeared in the Connecticut Gazette, while the British troops held possession of Boston. It was afterwards published in a ballad-sheet, and recently reproduced in Buckingham's Memoirs, its sentiment being a sufficient apology for the defects of the poetry.

A SONG.

SMILE, Massachusetts, smile,
Thy virtue still outbraves
The frowns of Britain's isle,
And rage of home-born slaves.
Thy free-born sons disdain their ease,
When purchased by their liberties.

Thy genius, once the pride
Of Britain's ancient isle,

Brought o'er the raging tide
By our forefather's toil;
In spite of North's despotic power,
Shines glorious on this western shore.

In Hancock's generous mind
Awakes the noble strife,
Which so conspicuous shined,
In gallant Sydney's life;
While in its cause the hero bled,
Immortal honors crown'd his head.

Let zeal your breasts inspire;
Let wisdom guide your plans;
'Tis not your cause entire,
On doubtful conflict hangs;
The fate of this vast continent,
And unborn millions share th' event.

To close the gloomy scenes
Of this alarming day,
A happy union reigns
Through wide America.

While awful wisdom hourly waits,
To adorn the councils of her states.

    Brave Washington arrives,
    Arrayed in warlike fame,
    While in his soul revives
    Great Marlboro's martial flame,
To lead your conquering armies on
To lasting glory and renown.

    To aid the glorious cause,
    Experienc'd Lee has come,
    Renown'd in foreign wars,
    A patriot at home.
While valiant Putnam's warlike deeds,
Amongst the foe a terror spreads.

    Let Britons proudly boast,
    " That their two thousand braves,
    Can drive our numerous host,
    And make us all their slaves ; "
While twice six thousand quake with fear,
Nor dare without their lines appear.

Kind Heaven has deign'd to own
Our bold resistance just,
Since murderous Gage began
The bloody carnage first.
Near ten to one has been their cost,
For each American we've lost.

Stand firm in your defence,
Like Sons of Freedom fight,
Your haughty foes convince,
That you'll maintain your right.
Defiance bid to tyrants' frown,
And glory will your valor crown.

Off from Boston.

1 7 7 6.

These congratulatory verses were sung by the soldiers of the Continental army, after the evacuation of Boston. It appeared under various names, but was generally known by its present title, or as the

MILITARY SONG.

Sons of valor, taste the glories
Of celestial liberty,
Sing a triumph [1] o'er the tories,
Let the pulse of joy beat high.

Heaven hath this day foil'd the many
  Fallacies of George the King;
Let the echo reach Britan'y,
  Bid her mountain summits ring.

See yon navy swell the bosom,
  Of the late enragèd sea;
Where'er they go, we shall oppose them,
  Sons of valor must be free.

Should they touch at fair Rhode Island,
  There to combat with the brave,
Driven from each dale and highland,
  They shall plough the purple wave

Should they thence to fair Virginia,
  Bend a squadron to Dunmore,
Still with fear and ignominy,
  They shall quit the hostile shore.

To Carolina or to Georg'y,
  Should they next advance their fame,
This land of heroes shall disgorge the
  Sons of tyranny and shame.

Let them rove to climes far distant,
    Situate under Arctic skies,
Call on Hessian troops [2] assistant,
    And the savages to rise.

Boast of wild brigades from Russia,
    To fix down the galling chain,
Canada and Nova Scotia,
    Shall disgorge these hordes again.

In New York state rejoin'd by Clinton,
    Should their standards mock the air,
Many a surgeon shall put lint on
    Wounds of death receivèd there.

War, fierce war, shall break their forces,
    Nerves of tory men shall fail,
Seeing Howe with alter'd courses,
    Bending to the western gale.

Thus from every bay òf ocean,
    Flying back with sails unfurl'd,
Tossed with ever-troubled motion,
    They shall quit this smiling world.

Like Satan banishèd from heaven,
   Never see the smiling shore;
From this land, so happy, driven,
   Never stain its bosom more.

[1] *Sing a triumph.* In February, 1776, Washington, who was at that time with the main army at Cambridge, proposed to a council of his officers, to cross upon the ice and attack the enemy, who held possession of Boston, but they unanimously disapproved of that daring scheme. It was, however, soon resolved to take possession of the heights of Dorchester; and on the morning of the fifth of March, the Americans had so far completed their works at that place, as to excite the astonishment of the ministerial troops, who evacuated Boston on the seventeenth of the same month. As the rear of the British army embarked, General Washington marched into the city, where he was joyfully received, as the " deliverer of his country."

[2] *Call on Hessian troops.* The British government "has sent over to Germany to engage troops for American service, and succeeded in raising a legion of Jagers, people brought up to the use of the rifle-barrel guns, in boar hunting. They are amazingly expert, and the ministry plume themselves much in the thought of their being a complete match for the American riflemen. We think they'll find boars in this country that will teach *them* how to grunt and wallow."

Freeman's Journal, 1776.

A Prayer.

1776.

The origin of this specimen of the "Yankee Psalms and Prayers" is unknown. There are numerous versions of it, but this is the only one that is above mediocrity, and suitable for this collection.

COMMON PRAYER FOR THE TIMES.

SINCE we are taught in Scripture word
    To pray for friends and foes;
Then let us pray for George the Third,
    Who must be one of those.

Heaven bless America, and Britain,
    May folly past suffice,
Wherein they have each other smitten,
    Who ought to harmonize.

Allied by blood, and interest too,
    Soon let them re-unite,
May Heaven tyrannic minds subdue,
    Haste, haste the pleasing sight.

May ev'ry morn and ev'ning prayer
    Repeat this just petition,
What thinking Christian can forbear,
    Appris'd of our condition.

Britannia's sins are our worst foes,
    Let this be Britain's creed,
For those who God and man oppose,
    Must rebels be indeed.

This rebel-host how num'rous grown !
    This growth kind Heaven forbid !
'Tis fear'd some are too near the throne,
    And seem securely hid.

Just Heaven, to light all rebels bring,
    Who hate or love the steeple.
Rebels to God, and to the king,
    And rebels to the people.

Burrowing Yankees.

1776.

This song must have been very popular with the loyalists, as four different editions were published in broadsides, during the two years following its first appearance, in the "Halifax Journal," a short time subsequent to the evacuation of Boston.

BURROWING YANKEES.[1]

Ye Yankees who, mole-like, still throw up the earth,
And like them, to your follies are blind from your birth;
Attempt not to hold British troops at defiance,
True Britons, with whom you pretend an alliance.

Mistake not; such blood ne'er run in your veins,
'Tis no more than the dregs, the lees, or the drains:
Ye affect to talk big of your hourly attacks;
Come on ! and I'll warrant, we'll soon see your backs.

Such threats of bravadoes serve only to warm
The true British hearts, you ne'er can alarm ;
The Lion once rous'd, will strike such a terror,
Shall show you, poor fools, your presumption and error.

And the time will soon come when your whole rebel race
Will be drove from the lands, nor dare show your face :
Here's a health to great *George*, may he fully determine,
To root from the earth all such insolent vermin.

[1] *Burrowing Yankees.* The newspapers, attached to the cause of the patriots, very generally republished this song as "a piece of tory gasconading." Among those, the editor of the "Freeman's Journal" reproduced it, congratulating his readers on having an opportunity to grace "Poet's corner, with an incomparable production" from a tory paper, at the same time observing, that the genius who wrote it, "must have forgotten the battles of Lexington and Bunker Hill."

𝕹𝖆𝖙𝖍𝖆𝖓 𝕳𝖆𝖑𝖊.

1776.

The particulars known, concerning the capture, trial, and execution of this gallant, and much lamented young officer, are few. Washington, after the retreat of his army from Long Island, in 1776, wishing to obtain information relative to the true situation, and intended operations, of the royal troops, applied to one of his officers, for a "discreet and enterprising person to penetrate the enemy's camp." This request was communicated to Nathan Hale,[1] a captain in Colonel Knowlton's regiment. "Animated by a sense of his duty," Hale undertook the dangerous service, and passed into the British lines in disguise. He obtained the desired information; but on his return, was apprehended and carried before Sir William Howe, to whom he frankly acknowledged the object of his visit. Howe immediately gave an order to the provost marshal, and Hale was executed in the early part of the next day. "The execution was carried on in a most unfeeling manner, and by as great a savage as ever disgraced humanity. A clergyman, whose attendance he desired, was refused him; a bible for a moment's devotion was not procured, though he requested it. Letters, which on the morning of his execution, he wrote to his mother, and other friends, were destroyed; and this very extraordinary reason given by the provost marshal, 'that the rebels should not know that they had a man in their army who could die with so much firmness.'" [2]

A BALLAD.

THE breezes went steadily thro' the tall pines,
　　A saying " oh ! hu-ush !" a saying " oh ! hu-ush !"
As stilly stole by a bold legion of horse,
　　For Hale in the bush, for Hale in the bush.

" Keep still !" said the thrush as she nestled her young,
　　In a nest by the road ; in a nest by the road.
" For the tyrants are near, and with them appear,
　　What bodes us no good, what bodes us no good."

The brave captain heard it, and thought of his home,
　　In a cot by the brook ; in a cot by the brook.
With mother and sister and memories dear,
　　He so gaily forsook ; he so gaily forsook.

Cooling shades of the night were coming apace,
　　The tattoo had beat ; the tattoo had beat.
The noble one sprang from his dark lurking place,
　　To make his retreat ; to make his retreat.

He warily trod on the dry rustling leaves,
  As he pass'd thro' the wood; as he pass'd thro' the
    wood;
And silently gain'd his rude launch on the shore,
  As she play'd with the flood; as she play'd with the
    flood.

The guards of the camp, on that dark, dreary night,
  Had a murderous will; had a murderous will.
They took him and bore him afar from the shore,
  To a hut on the hill; to a hut on the hill.

No mother was there, nor a friend who could cheer,
  In that little stone cell; in that little stone cell.
But he trusted in love, from his father above.
  In his heart, all was well; in his heart, all was well

An ominous owl with his solemn base voice,
  Sat moaning hard by; sat moaning hard by.
The tyrant's proud minions most gladly rejoice,
  "For he must soon die; for he must soon die."

The brave fellow told them, no thing he restrain'd,
  The cruel gen'ral; the cruel gen'ral.
His errand from camp, of the ends to be gain'd,
  And said that was all; and said that was all.

They took him and bound him and bore him away,
  Down the hill's grassy side; down the hill's grassy
    side.
'Twas there the base hirelings, in royal array,
  His cause did deride; his cause did deride.

Five minutes were given, short moments, no more,
  For him to repent; for him to repent;
He pray'd for his mother, he ask'd not another,
  To Heaven he went; to Heaven he went.

The faith of a martyr, the tragedy shew'd,
  As he trod the last stage; as he trod the last stage.
And Britons will shudder at gallant Hale's blood,
  As his words do presage, as his words do presage.

" Thou pale king of terrors, thou life's gloomy foe,
  Go frighten the slave, go frighten the slave;
Tell tyrants, to you, their allegiance they owe.
  No fears for the brave; no fears for the brave."

[1] *Nathan Hale* was a descendant of John Hale, first minister of
Beverly, Massachusetts. He was the son of Richard H. Hale, of
Coventry, Connecticut, and graduated at Yale College in 1773, with
high honors. Little is known of his private history. The subjoined

account of him is copied from the " Freeman's Journal," of February 18, 1777. " *The following is a genuine specimen of tory benevolence, and may be depended upon as real matter of fact.* Samuel Hale, late of Portsmouth, New Hampshire, after his elopement from thence, visited an uncle in Connecticut, where he was hospitably entertained ; but as his uncle was a whig, and had a son, a young gentleman of liberal education, and most amiable disposition, who strongly felt for his bleeding country, and being very active in the military way, was urged and prevailed on to take a commission in the Continental army ; consequently Samuel was obliged to conduct with caution, and counterfeit, as well as he could, a whiggish phiz, while he tarried, which was, however, but a short time, before he made his escape to General Howe in New York. Some time after this, Captain Hale, at the request of the General, went into New York in disguise, and having nearly accomplished his designs, who should he meet but his aforesaid cousin Samuel, whom he attempted to shun ; but Sam knew him too well. Captain Hale soon found he was advertised, and so particularly described, that he could not get through Long Island. He therefore attempted to escape by King's-bridge, and so far succeeded as to get to the outer guard, where he was suspected, apprehended, carried back and tried, and yet would have been acquitted, had not his affectionate and grateful cousin Samuel appeared and made oath, that he was a captain in the Continental army, and that he was in there as a spy, in consequence of which he was immediately hung up. However, at the gallows he made a sensible and spirited speech ; among other things told them they were shedding the blood of the innocent, and that if he had ten thousand lives, he would lay them all down, if called to it, in defence of this injured bleeding country.

" The printers throughout the continent are desired to exhibit this tragical scene to the public ; that they may see what they may expect if they fall into the hands of the tories."

[2] Hannah Adams' History of New England.

Sullivan's Island.

1 7 7 6 .

This ironical, and burlesque old song, was composed in the early
part of 1777. The author treats of the unsuccessful attack on Sullivan's Island, by the British, in the summer of the previous year,
and closes his epic with promises to gain lasting fame for the royal
arms, in all future actions. In the papers of the time, it appears as
a "New War Song, by Sir Peter Parker," written and printed in London, and adapted to the tune, " *Well met, brother Tar!*"

A NEW WAR SONG.

My Lords, with your leave,
An account I will give,[1]
That deserves to be written in metre:
For the rebels and I,
Have been pretty nigh,
Faith almost too nigh for Sir Peter.

With much labor and toil,
Unto Sullivan's Isle,[2]
I came firm as Falstaff or Pistol,
   But the Yankees, 'od rot 'em,
   I could not get at 'em :
Most terribly maul'd my poor Bristol.[3]

   Bold Clinton by land,[4]
   Did quietly stand,
While I made a thundering clatter;
   But the channel was deep,
   So he only could peep,
And not venture over the water.

   De'el take 'em, their shot
   Came so swift and so hot,
And the cowardly dogs [5] stood so stiff, sirs !
   That I put ship about,
   And was glad to get out,
Or they would not have left me a skiff, sirs !

   Now bold as a Turk,
   I proceed to New York,[6]
Where with Clinton and Howe you may find me.

I've the wind in my tail,

And am hoisting my sail,

To leave Sullivan's island behind me.

But my Lords, do not fear,

For before the next year,

Although a small island could fret us,

The Continent whole,

We shall take, by my soul,

If the cowardly Yankees [7] will let us.

[1] *An account I will give.* Late in the month of June, 1776, General Sir Henry Clinton, and Sir Peter Parker, with a powerful fleet and army, attempted the reduction of Charleston, South Carolina. The fleet came to anchor, at less than half musket shot from the fort on Sullivan's Island, and commenced the engagement. It lasted over ten hours, when the British were repulsed, after suffering great loss. After the firing ceased, the fleet slipped their cables, and before the next morning had retired two miles from the fort.

[2] *Sullivan's Isle* is situated on the northern side of Charleston harbor, about four miles from the town.

[3] *Most terribly maul'd my poor Bristol.* The Bristol flag-ship, under the command of Sir Peter Parker, was greatly damaged in the hull. Commodore Parker's breeches were torn off, his thigh and knee wounded, so that he walked only when supported on each side. The following extempore appeared in the Constitutional Gazette, at New York, a short time after this action.

> If "honor in the breech is lodged,"
> As Hudibras has shown,
> It may from thence be fairly judged,
> Sir Peter's honor gone.

⁴ *Bold Clinton by land.* General Clinton, some time before the engagement, landed with a number of troops on Long Island, and it was expected he would have co-operated with Sir Peter Parker, by crossing the narrow passage which divides the two islands; but Colonel Thompson with eight hundred men, stationed to oppose him, induced him to decline the perilous attempt.

⁵ *And the cowardly dogs.* The garrison under the command of Colonel Moultrie, although composed entirely of raw troops, showed determination and coolness that would have done honor to the oldest men in the service. They fired deliberately, for the most part took aim, and seldom missed their object. On the day after this gallant action, Moultrie cheered his officers and men in the following spirited and singular language: " *My brave companions,* you see the advantage of courage and fortitude. You have fought and have conquered, and the gallant fellows who fell in the cannonade of yesterday, are now in Heaven, riding in their chariots like the devil."

New Jersey Journal, 1779.

⁶ *I proceed to New York.* A few days after the engagement, the troops re-embarked and the whole sailed for New York.

⁷ *If the cowardly Yankees.* During the hottest fire of Sir Peter Parker's squadron, the flag of the fort was shot down. Sergeant William Jasper immediately stood upon the ramparts, with the flag in his hand, until another staff was handed to him, when he planted it and retired.

Independence.

1776.

This bold song appeared in the "Freeman's Journal," about one month previous to the declaration of independence, as a "Parody on an ode published in the Town and Country Magazine," in 1774. The loyal papers of the time speak of it as a specimen of "high-born rebel melody." There is a low and vulgar parody on this song, in a collection of "Fugitive Pieces," published at London in 1777.

INDEPENDENCE.

FREEMEN ! if you pant for glory,
If you sigh to live in story,
  If you burn with patriot zeal;
Seize this bright auspicious hour,
Chase those venal tools of power,
  Who subvert the public weal.

Huzza! Huzza! Huzza!
See Freedom her banner display,
Whilst glory and virtue your bosoms inspire,
Corruption's proud slaves shall with anguish retire.

Would traitors base with bribes beguile you,
Or with idiot scoffs revile you,
Ne'er your sacred trusts betray;
Hancock, Adams, nobly pleading,
Never from the truth receding,
Them, North's vengeance can't dismay.

See, their glorious path pursuing,
All Britannia's troops subduing,
Patriots whom no threats restrain.
Lawless tyrants all confounding,
Future times their praise resounding,
Shall their triumphs long maintain.

---

[1] *Freeman's Journal.* Among the newspapers foremost in support of the cause of the colonies, the "Freeman's Journal, or New Hampshire Gazette," published at Portsmouth, took a most decided and fearless position. No number of that paper appeared during that "well-tried contest," without some urgent appeal, filled with hope and encouragement for those who were struggling for their "rights and religion;" and its editors were ever faithful to their trusts and principles; never faltering to upbraid and oppose all who entertained any sympathy or affection for the British Government.

To the Commons.

1776.

This song was written in England, and first published in the Middlesex Journal, over the signature of M. On a broadside, dated 1777, the author says: "My efforts were so well received last year, I have the temerity to republish, in a more portable form, and try the royal brutes again. Heaven help us, if they will not take good advice, or stop for reflection, for they are speedily leading us to the ———."

TO THE COMMONS.

ON MEETING AFTER THE RECESS.

WITH Christmas mirth, and Christmas cheer,
    My friends pray look not glummer;
With turkey, chine, and beef and beer,
    You're surely in good humor.

The folks on t'other side the wave,
 Have beef as well as you, sirs;
Some chines, and turkeys too, they have,
 And as they bake they brew, sirs.

What, tho' your cannon raze their towns,
 And tumble down their houses,
They'll fight like devils [1] — blood and 'oons,
 For children and for spouses.

Another truth — nay, 'tis no boast,
 Nor yet the lie o' th' day, sirs;
The saints on Massachusetts coast,
 Gain if they run away, sirs.

For further than your bullets fly,
 A common man may run, sirs,
And wheat will grow beneath the sky,
 Where cannot reach a gun, sirs.

Then what are ships, and swords, and guns,
 And men of bloody mind, sirs,
While, Parthian-like, who conquers runs,
 Who loses,—stays behind, sirs.

Then rise my men, in merry mood,
  Vote — nem-con-tra-di-cente,
That five and five for ten are good,
  And ten and ten make twenty.

Recall your ships, your troops recall,
  Let friends each other nourish,
So shall old England rule the ball,
  And George and freedom flourish.

[1] *They'll fight like devils.* I see that the conduct of the New England peasantry has softened the hearts of some of our wise nobs, and that they dare to allow them a degree of " wisdom, courage, and bravery," although they have modified their praise slightly since the " dastard rebels" have gone to rhyming. Here's a fine specimen of " cowardice," by the last mail, from " loyal Virginia."

> " Let Britons, now sunk into tyrants and slaves !
> Submit to be governed by fools and by knaves.
> Not so will their kindred on this side the sea,
> American Britons will ever be free."
> *Note by author of the Song.*

On Independence.

1776.

The defiance and devotion expressed in these verses, are an excellent illustration of the spirit of the times, in which they were written. The author, Dr. Jonathan Mitchell Sewall,[1] of New Hampshire, composed many poems and patriotic songs. His ode of War and Washington is familiar to every one.

ON INDEPENDENCE.

Come all you brave soldiers, both valiant and free,
It's for Independence we all now agree;
Let us gird on our swords, and prepare to defend,
Our liberty, property, ourselves and our friends.

In a cause that's so righteous, come let us agree,
And from hostile invaders set America free,
The cause is so glorious we need not to fear,
But from merciless tyrants we'll set ourselves clear.

Heaven's blessing attending us, no tyrant shall say,
That Americans e'er to such monsters gave way,
But fighting we'll die in America's cause,
Before we'll submit to tyrannical laws.

George the Third, of Great Britain, no more shall he
     reign,
With unlimited sway o'er these free States again,
Lord North, nor old Bute, nor none of their clan,
Shall ever be honor'd by an American.

May Heaven's blessings descend on our United States,
And grant that the union may never abate;
May love, peace, and harmony, ever be found,
For to go hand in hand America round.

Upon our grand Congress may Heaven bestow,
Both wisdom and skill our good to pursue;
On Heaven alone dependent we'll be,
But from all earthly tyrants we mean to be free.

    7

Unto our brave Generals may Heaven give skill,
Our armies to guide, and the sword for to wield,
May their hands taught to war, and their fingers to fight,
Be able to put British armies to flight.

And now, brave Americans, since it is so,
That we are independent, we'll have them to know,
That united we are, and united we'll be,
And from all British tyrants we'll try to keep free.

May Heaven smile on us in all our endeavors,
Safe guard our seaports, our towns, and our rivers,
Keep us from invaders by land and by sea,
And from all who'd deprive us of our liberty.

[1] *Jonathan M. Sewall* was born in 1749. Being adopted by his uncle, Chief Justice Stephen Sewall, of Massachusetts, he studied law, and in 1774 was Register of Probate for Grafton County, N. H. He afterwards removed to Portsmouth, where he died March 29, 1808. — *Allen's Biographical Dictionary.*

A Ballad.

1 7 7 6.

TO THE TUNE OF "SMILE BRITANNIA."

RISE, rise, bright genius rise,
Conduct thy sons to war;
Thy spear pois'd to the skies,
Whirl, whirl, thy rapid car;
Fire each firm breast with noble zeal,
To conquer for the common weal.

For years the iron rod,
Has hover'd o'er our heads,
Submit to George's nod,
Whose power all Europe dreads;
The slavish minion trembling cries,
But freedom's sons all fears despise.

All means for peace we've tried,
But found those measures vain,
North's ministerial pride,
Thought fear made us complain ·
But in the end convinc'd he'll see,
We dread not death, but slavery.

Tho' fatal lust of power,
Has steel'd the tyrant's soul,
Tho' in an ill-timed hour,
He bid his thunders roll,
Great Liberty, inspir'd by thee,
We fly to death or victory !

Great nature's law inspires,
All free-born souls unite,
While common interest fires
Us to defend our rights,
Against corruption's boundless claim,
And firmly fix great freedom's reign.

They foreign troops employ,
For mercenary hire;

Their weakness we enjoy,
Each pulse rew ardors fire ;
Convinc'd the wretch who fights for pay,
Will never bear the palm away.

They boast their power by sea,
The ruin of our trade,
Our navy soon they'll see,
Wide o'er the ocean spread ;
Britain not long shall boast her reign,
O'er the wide empire of the main.

Throughout the universe,
Our commerce we'll extend,
Each power on the reverse,
Shall seek to be our friends,
Whilst our sons, crown'd with wealth immense,
Sing Washington and Common Sense.

𝕭𝖆𝖙𝖙𝖑𝖊 𝖔𝖋 𝕿𝖗𝖊𝖓𝖙𝖔𝖓.

1 7 7 6.

Numerous songs, odes, epigrams and pasquinades, commemorating this battle, appeared during the war. We have several loyal
productions upon this subject; but they are too profane and corrupt
for publication at the present time. The author of the one subjoined
is unknown. The Earl Dorset's lyric "Fire of Love," which was
very popular at the period of the Revolution, is, probably, the song
upon which this was modelled.

BATTLE OF TRENTON.[1]

ON Christmas day in seventy-six,
Our ragged troops with bayonets fix'd,
 For Trenton marched away.
The Delaware see! the boats below!
The light obscured by hail and snow!
 But no signs of dismay.

Our object was the Hessian band,
That dared invade fair freedom's land,
    And quarter in that place.
Great Washington he led us on,
Whose streaming flag, in storm or sun,
    Had never known disgrace.

In silent march we pass'd the night,
Each soldier panting for the fight,
    Though quite benumb'd with frost.
Greene, on the left, at six began,
The right was led by Sullivan,
    Who ne'er a moment lost.

Their pickets storm'd, the alarm was spread,
That rebels risen from the dead
    Were marching into town.
Some scamper'd here, some scamper'd there,[2]
And some for action did prepare ;
    But soon their arms laid down.

Twelve hundred servile miscreants,
With all their colors,[3] guns, and tents,
    Were trophies of the day.

The frolic o'er, the bright canteen,
In centre, front, and rear was seen
   Driving fatigue away.

Now, brothers of the patriot bands,
Let's sing deliverance from the hands
   Of arbitrary sway.
And as our life is but a span,
Let's touch the tankard while we can,
   In memory of that day.

[1] *Battle of Trenton.* Curiosities of American Literature, by Rufus W. Griswold.

[2] *Some scamper'd there.* "It is said some Hessian officers and other mercenaries, were greatly disturbed one morning, at Trenton, when they waked up and found rebels knocking in their doors."

[3] *With all their colors.* "On the Hessian standards taken at Trenton, were the words: '*Nescit Pericula*,'—a fearlessness of danger,—which was not displayed in the battle where the standards were surrendered, and which hath drawn on the timid Hessian, and his vaunting motto, the following epigram:

"The man who submits without striking a blow,
  May be said, in a sense, no danger to know:
  I pray then, what harm, by the humble submission,
  At Trenton was done by the standard of Hessian?'"

                                         N. H. Gazette.

𝕿𝖍𝖊 𝕳𝖊𝖆𝖉𝖘 :

OR THE YEAR.

1776.

This song was probably written in England. There were several versions of it published in this country. We select the best.

THE HEADS.

Y<small>E</small> wrong heads, and strong heads attend to my strains ;
Y<small>e</small> clear heads, and queer heads, and heads without
    brains ;
Y<small>e</small> thick skulls, and quick skulls, and heads great and
    small ;
And ye heads that aspire to be heads over all.
      Derry down, down, hey derry down.

7*

Ye ladies—I would not offend for the world,
Whose bright heads, and light heads, are feather'd and
  curl'd;
The mighty dimensions dame Nature surprise,
To find she'd so grossly mistaken the size.

And ye petit-maitres, your heads I might spare,
Encumber'd with nothing—but powder and hair;
Who vainly disgrace the true monkey race,
By transplanting the tail from its own native place.

Enough might be said, durst I venture my rhymes,
On crown'd heads, and round heads, of these modern
  times;
This slippery path let me cautiously tread—
The neck else may answer, perhaps, for the head.

The heads of the church, and the heads of the state,
Have taught much, and wrought much,—too much to
  repeat;
On the neck of corruption uplifted, 'tis said,
Some rulers, alas! are too high by the head.

Ye schemers and dreamers of politic things,
Projecting the downfall of kingdoms and kings;
Can your wisdom declare how this body is fed,
When the members rebel and wage war with the head?

Expounders, confounders, and heads of the law,
I bring case in point, do not point out a flaw;
If reason is treason, what plea shall I plead?
To your chief I appeal—for your chief has a head.

On Britannia's bosom sweet Liberty smil'd,
The parent grew strong while she foster'd the child,
Neglecting her offspring, a fever she bred,
Which contracted her limbs, and distracted her head.

Ye learnèd state doctors, your labors are vain,
Proceeding by bleeding to settle her brain;
Much less can your art the lost members restore,
Amputation must follow—perhaps something more.

Pale Goddess of Whim! when with cheeks lean or full,
Thy influence seizes an Englishman's skull,
He blunders, yet wonders his schemes ever fail,
Tho' often mistaking the head for the tail.

   Derry down, down, hey derry down.

The Jerseys.

1776.

This parody on the "Watery God" was occasioned by the success of the Americans at Trenton and Princeton. It was published a short time after those victories, and soon became a favorite.

A PARODY.

As Mars, great god of battles! lay,
In dalliance soft and amorous play,
    On fair Bellona's breast;
Surpris'd he rear'd his hoary head,
The conscious goddess shook with dread,
    And all her fears confess'd.

Loud thunder roll'd through Heaven's domain,
The ethereal world was wrapt in flame,

    The god amazèd spoke :
Go forth, ye powers, and make it known,
Who dares thus boldly shake my throne,

    And fill my realms with smoke.

The gods, obsequious to his word,
Sprang swiftly forth t' obey their lord,

    And saw two hosts away;
The one, great Washington, was thine;
The other, Howe's disordered line,

    In sorrow and dismay.

Appall'd they view'd Columbia's sons,
Deal death and slaughter from their guns,

    And strike a dreadful blow,
Which made ill-fated British slaves,
On distant shores to find their graves,

    And sink to shades below.

Amaz'd they tell of battles won,
That Britain's ruin'd; Washington

    Alone triumphant rode;

Ha ! cries the fair, pray who is he
That dare's reverse e'en Jove's decree,
 And thus insult a god ?

The gods reply, in yonder lands,
Great Liberty alone commands,
 And gives the hero force ;
And when his thundering cannon roar,
And strike with dread earth's distant shore,
 'Tis she directs their course.

And when her wingèd bullets fly,
To check a tyrant's treachery,
 And lay his glories low;
Then Washington serenely great,
Tho' death and carnage round him wait,
 Performs the dreadful blow.

The god with wonder heard the story,
Astonish'd view'd Columbia's glory,
 Which time can ne'er subdue,
Great Warren's deeds, and Gates's fame,
Join'd to great Lee's immortal name ;[1]
 And cried, Can this be true ?

Britain shall cease to plague mankind,
With sister tyrants strive to bind,

And check the free-born soul;
To Washington her trophies yield,
Freedom shall triumph in the field,

And rule from pole to pole.

[1] *Lee's immortal name.* General Charles Lee was taken prisoner in 1776 while marching through New Jersey to join General Washington, and was not exchanged until 1778. This song was written while he remained with the British.

The Prophetic Egg.

1777.

The following lines appeared in the early part of 1777, with this introduction. "As the superstition and weakness of human nature is such, that sometimes the most trivial circumstance ; or grossest absurdity is attended with serious consequences, we acquaint the timid and credulous, that characters inscribed on adamant are much more durable than when wrote only on an egg-shell. And also inform the public, that about the time the prophetic egg was laid in the town of Plymouth, with this wonderful prediction wrote on its shell, "*Oh, oh, America, Howe shall be thy conqueror*," a hermit, resembling the Genius of America, who had resided in a certain forest from the first settlement of the country, found the following lines inscribed on a fragment of marble near his cave, visited by the curious from all parts of Europe, for the remarkable echo, which oft reverberated in loud peals, heard beyond the Atlantic."

ANOTHER PROPHECY.[1]

BRITANNIA sinks beneath her crimes,
She dies — she dies — let empire rise,
And freedom cheer the western skies.

When every art and menace fails,
And Tory lies and Tory tales,
Are universally abhorr'd,
They now pretend to fear the Lord.
Instead of virtue, a long face;
Instead of piety, grimace;
Pretend strange revelation given,
And intimation sent from Heaven.

To carry on the schemes of Bute,
A speaking egg they substitute.
A strange phenomenon indeed,
The stratagem must sure succeed;
And every mortal die with fear,
When they the sad prediction hear.

The egg was laid without the tent,
Ergo, it was from Heaven sent.
The egg was found within a barn,
Ergo, from it, we surely learn,
When eggs can speak what fools indite,
And hens can talk as well as write,
When crocodiles shed honest tears,
And truth with hypocrites appears;
When every man becomes a knave,
And feels the spirit of the slave;

And when veracity again,
Shall in a Tory's bosom reign;
When vice is virtue, darkness light,
And freemen are afraid to fight;
When they forget to play the men,
And with the spirit of a hen,
Desert the just and sacred cause;
And opening Heaven smiles applause
On such a bloody, barbarous foe,
Then I'll be conquered by a Howe.

[1] *Another prophecy.* The credulity of the ignorant was often imposed on by the advocates of both parties, during the revolution. The following extract from a letter, written a short time after the battle at Trenton, will explain itself. "The enemy appear to be panic-struck in the extreme. God prospers our arms in an extraordinary manner. There is to be an eclipse of the sun to-day, and we mean, if possible, to attack the Germans as soon as it begins, and take advantage of their ignorant superstition."

To Britain.

1 7 7 7 .

The following bold lines are taken from the "Craftsman, or Say's British Journal." The American newspapers, both loyal and whig, generally republished them.

TO BRITAIN.

BLUSH Britain ! blush at thy inglorious war,
This civil contest, this ignoble jar;
Think how unjustly you've begun the fray,
With cruel measures rous'd America.

To arms : each swain must leave the peaceful field,
And 'gainst his brethren lift the sword and shield.
Their spacious commerce, now in ruin lies,
And thro' their land the hostile standard flies.

Britain, what laurel canst thou hope to gain?
Can any action give a hero fame?
In brother's blood our soldiers' hands imbru'd,
And barb'rous hostiles by our chiefs pursu'd.

Afflicting Britain, thus to spoil thy name,
Defeat's a scandal, conquest but a shame.
Our senators all lost in dire excess,
Lovers of pleasure, luxury, and dress.

Almighty ruler, stretch thy potent hand,
And o'er Britannia wave the olive wand;
Preserve our nation from th' impending fate,
Drive clouds of Scotchmen from the British state;
Fair peace descend, with all thy prosp'rous train,
And spread thy blessings o'er our spacious plain.

General Sullivan's Song.

1777.

This song "was sung before General Sullivan and a few respectable gentlemen, at Portsmouth, New Hampshire, after the battle of Trenton."

GENERAL SULLIVAN'S SONG.

HARK, the loud drums, hark, the shrill trumpet-call to
    arms,
Come, Americans come, prepare for war's alarms,
       Whilst in array we stand,
       What soldier dare to land,
     Sure in the attempt to meet his doom,
     A leaden death, or a watery tomb;

We, Americans, so brave, o'er the land or the waves,
All invaders defy, we'll repulse them or die,
      We scorn to live as slaves.

Recall the days, wherein our fathers bravely fought,
And crown'd with praise, they patriot glory sought,
      Bid their high deeds inspire,
      Bid Magna Charta fire,
    Greatly they labor'd for our good
    All sorts of tyranny withstood,
All these we despise, on our courage rely,
For what American so base would his country disgrace
      And from his colors fly.

No party spite, no more our measures will oppose,
For all unite against our insulting foes,
      All then in chorus sing,
      And let your voices ring,
    Fill unto Sullivan the flowing bowl,
    Hand it to each gallant soul,
Raise patriot flame, his glory proclaim
Who his sword boldly draws in his country's cause,
      And wins an endless name.

The Proclamation.

1777.

On the fourth of July, 1777, General Burgoyne issued a proclamation from his camp, near Ticonderoga, intended to spread terror among the Americans. But it was so pompous and bombastic, that, instead of producing the desired effect, it became the subject of ridicule and derision. The subjoined version of it, is attributed to Francis Hopkinson.

BURGOYNE'S PROCLAMATION.

By John Burgoyne, and Burgoyne, John, Esq.,
And grac'd with titles still more higher,[1]
For I'm Lieutenant-general, too,
Of George's troops both red and blue,
On this extensive continent;
And of Queen Charlotte's regiment

Of light dragoons the Colonel;
And Governor eke of Castle Wil—
And furthermore, when I am there,
In House of Commons I appear,
[Hoping ere long to be a Peer.]
Being a member of that virtuous band
Who always vote at North's command;
Directing too the fleet and troops
From Canada as thick as hops;
And all my titles to display,
I'll end with thrice et cetera.

The troops consign'd to my command
Like Hercules to purge the land,
Intend to act in combination
With th' other forces of the nation,
Displaying wide thro' every quarter
What Britain's justice would be after.
It is not difficult to show it,
And every mother's son must know it,
That what she meant at first to gain
By requisitions and chicane,
She's now determin'd to acquire
By kingly reason; sword and fire.

I can appeal to all your senses,
Your judgments, feelings, tastes and fancies;
Your ears and eyes have heard and seen,
How causeless this revolt has been;
And what a dust your leaders kick up;
In this rebellious civil hickup,
And how, upon this curs'd foundation,
Was rear'd the system of vexation
Over a stubborn generation.

But now inspired with patriot love
I come th' oppression to remove;
To free you from the heavy clog
Of every tyrant demagogue.
Who for the most romantic story,
Claps into limbo loyal Tory,
All hurly burly, hot and hasty,
Without a writ to hold him fast by;
Nor suffers any living creature,
[Led by the dictates of his nature,]
To fight in green for Britain's cause,
Or aid us to restore her laws;
In short, the vilest generation
Which in vindictive indignation,

8

Almighty vengeance ever hurl'd
From this to the infernal world.
A Tory cannot move his tongue,
But whip, in prison he is flung,
His goods and chattels made a prey.
By those vile mushrooms of a day,
He's tortur'd too, and scratch'd and bit,
And plung'd into a dreary pit;
Where he must suffer sharper doom,
Than e'er was hatched by Church of Rome.
These things are done by rogues, who dare
Profess to breathe in Freedom's air.
To petticoats alike and breeches
Their cruel domination stretches,
For the sole crime, or sole suspicion
[What worse is done by th' inquisition?]
Of still adhering to the crown,
Their tyrants striving to kick down,
Who by perverting law and reason,
Allegiance construe into treason.
Religion too is often made
A stalking horse to drive the trade,
And warring churches dare implore,
Protection from th' Almighty pow'r;

They fast and pray : in Providence
Profess to place their confidence;
And vainly think the Lord of all
Regards our squabbles on this ball ;
Which would appear as droll in Britain
As any whim that one could hit on ;
Men's consciences are set at naught,
Nor reason valued at a groat ;
And they that will not swear and fight,
Must sell their all, and say good night.

   By such important views there pres't to,
I issue this my manifesto.
I, the great knight of de la Mancha,
Without 'Squire Carleton, my Sancho,
Will tear you limb from limb asunder,
With cannon, blunderbuss and thunder;
And spoil your feathering and your tarring;
And cagg you up for pickled herring.
In front of troops as spruce as beaux,
And ready to lay on their blows,
I'll spread destruction far and near ;
And where I cannot kill, I'll spare,
Inviting, by these presents, all,
Both young and old, and great and small,

And rich and poor, and Whig and Tory,
In cellar deep, or lofty story ;
Where'er my troops at my command
Shall swarm like locusts o'er the land.
(And they shall march from the North Pole
As far, at least, as Pensacole,)
So break off their communications,
That I can save their habitations ;
For finding that Sir William's plunders,
Prove in the event apparent blunders,
It is my full determination,
To check all kinds of depredation ;
But when I've got you in my pow'r,
Favor'd is he, I last devour.

From him who loves a quiet life,
And keeps at home to kiss his wife,
And drinks success to king Pigmalion,
And calls all Congresses Rabscallion,
With neutral stomach eats his supper,
Nor deems the contest worth a copper ;
I will not defalcate a groat,
Nor force his wife to cut his throat ;
But with his doxy he may stay,
And live to fight another day ;

Drink all the cider he has made,
And have to boot, a green cockade.
But as I like a good Sir Loin,
And mutton chop whene'er I dine,
And my poor troops have long kept Lent,
Not for religion, but for want,
Whoe'er secretes cow, bull or ox,
Or shall presume to hide his flocks;
Or with felonious hand eloign
Pig, duck, or gosling from Burgoyne,
Or dare to pull the bridges down,
My boys to puzzle or to drown;
Or smuggle hay, or plough, or harrow,
Cart, horses, wagons or wheelbarrow;
Or 'thwart the path, lay straw or switch,
As folks are wont to stop a witch,
I'll hang him as the Jews did Haman;
And smoke his carcase for a gammon.
I'll pay in coin for what I eat,
Or Continental counterfeit.
But what's more likely still, I shall
(So fare my troops,) not pay at all.

   With the most Christian spirit fir'd,
And by true soldiership inspir'd,

I speak as men do in a passion
To give my speech the more impression.
If any should so harden'd be,
As to expect impunity,
Because procul a fulmine,
I will let loose the dogs of Hell,
Ten thousand Indians, who shall yell,
And foam and tear, and grin and roar,
And drench their moccasins in gore ;
To these I'll give full scope and play
From Ticonderog to Florida ;
They'll scalp your heads, and kick your shins,
And rip your ——, and flay your skins,
And of your ears be nimble croppers,
And make your thumbs tobacco-stoppers.
If after all these loving warnings,
My wishes and my bowels' yearnings,
You shall remain as deaf as adder,
Or grow with hostile rage the madder,
I swear by George, and by St. Paul
I will exterminate you all.
Subscrib'd with my manual sign
To test these presents, John Burgoyne.

¹ *Titles still more higher.* In his proclamation the General announced himself as "John Burgoyne, Esq., Lieutenant-general of his Majesty's armies in America, Colonel of the Queen's regiment of light dragoons, Governor of fort William in North Britain, one of the representatives of the Commons of Great Britain in Parliament, and commanding an army and fleet employed on an expedition from Canada, &c. &c. &c." On the surrender of the British army in the autumn of 1777, Governor William Livingston, of New Jersey, proposed to exchange Burgoyne, "in such a manner as would, at the same time, flatter his vanity, and redound to the greatest emolument of America." He proposed to detain him until "we can get in exchange for him, one Esquire, two Major-generals, three Colonels of light horse, two Governors, one member of Congress, the Admiral of our navy, one Commander-in-chief, in a separate department, and six privates."

Saratoga Song.

1777.

This ballad was known during the revolution, as the " North Campaign," " Gates' Song," and " A Song for the Red-Coats." It has been attributed to a " private of Colonel Brook's regiment," [1] and also to the author of " American Taxation."

A SONG FOR THE RED-COATS.

Come unto me ye heroes
    Whose hearts are true and bold,
Who value more your honor,
    Than others do their gold;
Give ear unto my story,
    And I the truth will tell,
Concerning many a soldier,
    Who for his country fell.

Burgoyne, the king's commander,
    From Canada set sail,
With full eight thousand reg'lars,
    He thought he could not fail;
With Indians and Canadians,
    And his curs'd Tory crew,
On board his fleet of shipping,
    He up the Champlain flew.

Before Ticonderoga,
    The first day of July,
Appear'd his ships and army,
    And we did them espy.
Their motions we observèd,
    Full well both night and day,
And our brave boys preparèd,
    To have a bloody fray.

Our garrison they viewed them,
    And straight their troops did land,
And when St. Clair, our chieftain,
    The fact did understand,

8*

That they the Mount Defiance
Were bent to fortify,
He found we must surrender,
Or else prepare to die.

The fifth day of July, then,
He ordered a retreat,
And when next morn we started,
Burgoyne thought we were beat.
And closely he pursued us,
Till when near Hubbardton,
Our rear guards were defeated,
He thought the country won.

And when 'twas told in Congress,
That we our forts had left,
To Albany retreated,
Of all the North bereft;
Brave General Gates they sent us,
Our fortunes to retrieve,
And him with shouts of gladness,
The army did receive.

Where first the Mohawk's waters.
　　Do in the sunshine play,
For Herkimer's brave soldiers,
　　Sellinger [2] ambush'd lay ;
And them he there defeated,
　　But soon he had his due,
And scared by Brooks and Arnold,
　　He to the north withdrew.

To take the stores and cattle,
　　That we had gather'd then,
Burgoyne sent a detachment
　　Of fifteen hundred men ;
By Baum they were commanded,
　　To Bennington they went ;
To plunder and to murder,
　　Was fully their intent.

But little did they know then,
　　With whom they had to deal,
It was not quite so easy,
　　Our stores and stock to steal ;

Bold Stark would give them only,
   A portion of his lead ;
With half his crew ere sunset,
   Baum lay among the dead.

The nineteenth of September,
   The morning cool and clear,
Brave Gates rode through our army,
   Each soldier's heart to cheer ;
" Burgoyne," he cried, " advances,
   But we will never fly ;
No — rather than surrender,
   We'll fight him till we die."

The news was quickly brought us,
   The enemy was near,
And all along our lines then
   There was no signs of fear ;
It was above Stillwater
   We met at noon that day,
And every one expected
   To see a bloody fray.

Six hours the battle lasted,
    Each heart was true as gold,
The British fought like lions,
    And we like Yankees bold;
The leaves with blood were crimson,
    And then brave Gates did cry —
" 'Tis diamond now cut diamond!
    We'll beat them boys or die."

The darkness soon approaching,
    It forced us to retreat,
Into our lines till morning,
    Which made them think us beat;
But ere the sun was risen,
    They saw before their eyes,
Us ready to engage them,
    Which did them much surprise.

Of fighting they seem weary,
    Therefore to work they go,
Their thousand dead to bury,
    And breastworks up to throw;

With grape and bombs intending
> Our army to destroy,
Or from our works our forces
> By stratagem decoy.

The seventh day of October,
> The British tried again,
Shells from their cannons throwing,
> Which fell on us like rain;
To drive us from our stations,
> That they might thus retreat;
For now Burgoyne saw plainly,
> He never could us beat.

But vain was his endeavor
> Our men to terrify;
Though death was all around us,
> Not one of us would fly.
But when an hour we'd fought them,
> And they began to yield,
Along our lines the cry ran,
> " The next blow wins the field !"

Great God, who guides their battles,
 Whose cause is just and true,
Inspire our bold commander,
 The course he should pursue.
He ordered Arnold forward,
 And Brooks to follow on ;
The enemy was routed !
 Our liberty was won !

Then burning all their luggage,
 They fled with haste and fear,
Burgoyne with all his forces,
 To Saratogue did steer ;
And Gates, our brave commander,
 Soon after him did hie,
Resolving he would take them,
 Or in the effort die.

As we came nigh the village,
 We overtook the foe ;
They'd burned each house to ashes,
 Like all where'er they go.

The seventeenth of October,
　　They did capitulate,
Burgoyne and his proud army,
　　Did we our pris'ners make.

Now, here's a health to Arnold,
　　And our commander Gates,
To Lincoln and to Washington,
　　Whom every Tory hates;
Likewise unto our Congress,
　　God grant it long to reign;
Our Country, Right, and Justice,
　　For ever to maintain.

Now finish'd is my story,
　　My song is at an end;
The freedom we're enjoying
　　We're ready to defend;
For while our cause is righteous,
　　Heaven nerves the soldier's arm,
And vain is their endeavor,
　　Who strive to do us harm.

[1] Curiosities of American Literature, by Rufus W. Griswold, page 32.

[2] *St. Leger*, pronounced Sellinger.

A Song.

1777.

A very few ballads were published during the year 1777. "For some reason the muse is asleep," says the editor of the New Jersey Journal, shortly after the defeat of Burgoyne.

THE FATE OF JOHN BURGOYNE.

When Jack, the King's commander,
　　Was going to his duty,
Through all the crowd he smil'd and bow'd,
　　To every blooming beauty.

The city rung with feats he'd done,
　　In Portugal and Flanders,
And all the town thought he'd be crown'd
　　The first of Alexanders.

To Hampton Court he first repairs,
    To kiss great George's hand, sirs,
Then to harangue on state affairs,
    Before he left the land, sirs.

The "lower house" sat mute as mouse,
    To hear his grand oration;
And "all the peers" with loudest cheers,
    Proclaim'd him to the nation.

Then off he went to Canada,
    Next to Ticonderoga,
And quitting those, away he goes,
    Straightway to Saratoga.

With great parade his march he made,
    To gain his wished for station,
When far and wide his minions hied,
    To spread his " Proclamation."

To such as staid he offers made,
    Of " pardon on submission;
But savage bands should waste the lands
    Of all in opposition."

But ah, the cruel fate of war !
   This boasted son of Britain,
When mounting his triumphal car,
   With sudden fear was smitten.

The sons of freedom gathered round,
   His hostile bands confounded,
And when they'd fain have turn'd their back,
   They found themselves surrounded !

In vain they fought, in vain they fled,
   Their chief, humane and tender,
To save the rest, soon thought it best
   His forces to surrender.

Brave St. Clair when he first retired,
   Knew what the fates portended ;
And Arnold and heroic Gates,
   His conduct have defended.

Thus may America's brave sons
   With honor be rewarded,
And be the fate of all her foes,
   The same as here recorded.

𝔅𝔲𝔯𝔤𝔬𝔶𝔫𝔢'𝔰 ℭ𝔟𝔢𝔯𝔱𝔥𝔯𝔬𝔴.

1777.

This poetical "army return" was first published in the "Iris," (June, 1841,) from the original MS. in the possession of GEORGE H. MOORE, one of the editors of that periodical. It is a resumé of the losses of the British army during the northern campaign which terminated at Saratoga, and, as will be noticed by the reader, gives the results in round numbers.

BURGOYNE'S OVERTHROW AT SARATOGA.

HERE followeth the direful fate
Of Burgoyne and his army great,
Who so proudly did display
The terrors of despotic sway.
His power, and pride, and many threats,
Have been brought low by fort'nate Gates,
To bend to the United States.

British prisoners by Convention,   .   .   .   2442

Foreigners—by Contra-vention,   .   .   .   2198

Tories sent across the Lake,   .   .   .   1100

Burgoyne and suite, in state,   .   .   .   12

Sick and wounded, bruised and pounded, ⎫
                                                                                        ⎬   528
Ne'er so much before confounded,   ⎭

Prisoners of war before Convention,   .   .   400

Deserters come with kind intention,   .   .   300

They lost at Bennington's great battle,   ⎫
                                                                                    ⎬   1220
Where glorious Starke's arms did rattle, ⎭

Killed in September and October,.   .   .   600

Ta'en by brave Brown, some drunk, some sober,   413

Slain by high-famed Herkerman,⎫
                                                                        ⎬   300
On both flanks, on rear and van,⎭

Indians, suttlers, and drovers,   ⎤
                                                                                        |
Enough to crowd large plains all over, |
                                                                                        |
And those whom grim Death did prevent |
                                                                                        ⎬   4413
From fighting against our continent; |
                                                                                        |
And also those who stole away, |
                                                                                        |
Lest down their arms they should lay, |
                                                                                        |
Abhorring that obnoxious day;   ⎦

The whole make fourteen thousand men, ⎫
                                                                                    ⎬   14,000
Who may not with us fight again,   ⎭

This is a pretty just account
Of Burgoyne's legions whole amount,
Who came across the Northern Lakes
To desolate our happy States.
Their brass cannons we have got all—
Fifty-six—both great and small;
And ten thousand stand of arms,
To prevent all future harms;
Stores and implements complete,
Of workmanship exceeding neat;
Covered wagons in great plenty,
And proper harness, no way scanty.
Among our prisoners there are
Six Generals, of fame most rare;
Six members of their Parliament—
Reluctantly they seem content;
Three British Lords, and Lord Bellcaras,
Who came, our country free to harass.
Two Barouets of high extraction,
Were sorely wounded in the action.

The Gamester.

1778.

The defeat of General Burgoyne caused great alarm and uneasiness in England. Parliament soon after that event sent commissioners to the Continental Congress, with proposals for a mutual adjustment of the existing difficulties, couched in the most conciliatory and plausible terms, and calculated to occasion disaffection among the people of the colonies, who, in many instances were becoming disheartened and tired of the war. Fearing such an event, Congress immediately published an address, wherein they fully exposed the snare prepared by the royal commissioners; and, at the same time, encouraged the patriots with the brightest prospect of success, in the final establishment of their liberty and independence. This address had the desired effect. The people resolved not to be deceived. The following ballad appeared before the royal commissioners returned to England, in a double-columned sheet, adapted to the tune, "A late worthy old Lion."

A NEW SONG.

WEST of the old Atlantic, firm Liberty stands!
Hov'ring Fame just alighted, supported by bands

Of natives free born, who loud echoing sing,
" We'll support our just rights 'gainst tyrannic kings ! "
    Caral-laddy—caral-laddy, &c.

George the Third she disowns and his proud lordly cheats,
His murdering legions and half-famish'd fleets ;
To the Jerseys sneak'd off, with fear quite dismay'd,
Although they much boasted, that fighting's their trade.

Our just rights to assert, hath the Congress oft tried,
Whose wisdom and strength our opponents deride,
And still madly in rage their weak thunders are hurl'd,
To bring us on our knees and to bully the world.

Too haughty to yield, yet too weak to withstand,
They skulk to their ships and leave us the firm land ;
In dread lest they share what Jack Burgoyne did feel,
And the game be quite lost, as poor Jack had lost deal.

Jack, thinking of cribbage, all fours, or of put,
With a dexterous hand, he did shuffle and cut,
And when likely to lose—like a sharper they say—
Did attempt to renege—I mean, run away.

But watch'd so closely, he could not play booty,
Yet to cheat he fain would, for George—'twas his duty;
A great bet depending on that single game;
Dominion and honor—destruction and shame.

Examin'd with care his most critical hand,
At a loss, if better to beg or to stand,
His tricks reckon'd up; for all sharpers can jangle;
Then kick'd up a dust, for his favorite wrangle.

'Twas diamond cut diamond, spades were of no use,
But to dig up the way for surrender and truce;
For he dreaded the hand that dealt out such thumps;
As the hearts were run out, and clubs were then trumps.

Thus he met with the rubbers, as the game it turn'd out,
Poor Jack, although beat, made a damnable rout,
Complain'd he was cheated,[1] and pompously talks;
Quit the game with a curse, while he rubb'd out the
    chalks.

But see a cloud burst, and a seraph appears,
Loud trumpeting peace, while in blood to their ears,
With bulls and with pardons for us on submission;
To bull us, and gull us, by their sham commission.
9

The haughty great George then to peace is now prone;
A bully when matched soon can alter his tone;
'Tis the act of a Briton to bluster and threaten;
Hangs his tail like a spaniel, when handsomely beaten.

Charge your glasses lip high, to brave Washington sing,
To the union so glorious the whole world shall ring;
May their councils in wisdom and valor unite,
And the men[2] ne'er be wrong, who yet so far are right.

The great Doctor Franklin the next glass must claim,
Whose electrical rod strikes terror and shame;
Like Moses, who caused Pharaoh's heart-strings to
    grumble,
Shock'd George on his throne, his magicians made humble.

To Gates and to Arnold, with bumpers we'll join,
And to all our brave troops who took gambling Burgoyne.
May their luck still increase, as they've turn'd up one
    Jack,
To cut and turn up all the knaves in the pack.[3]

[1] *Complained he was cheated, and pompously talks.* "Though the articles of convention were fully adjusted, signed and exchanged, by those appointed for the purpose, and the hour stipulated by the par-

ties for Burgoyne to affix his signature, he addressed a note to General Gates, purporting that he should recede from the treaty, on the ground that a part of the American force had been detached from the army during the negotiation; and with a bold effrontery, required, that he might be permitted to send two officers to the American camp to ascertain the fact. This dishonorable conduct raised the ire of General Gates, who sent Lieutenant-colonel Wilkinson to insist that hostilities would recommence if the treaty was not immediately ratified. This produced the desired effect."

Thacher's Journal.

[2] *And the men.* The Continental Congress, in all their acts, were unanimously supported by the patriots.

[3] *To cut and turn up all the knaves in the pack.* The Earl of Dartmouth asked an American in London, of how many members the Congress consisted? To which the reply was "fifty-two." "Why, that is the number of cards in a pack," said his lordship, "pray how many *knaves* are there?" "Not one," returned the republican, "please to recollect that *knaves* are *court* cards."

The Rebels.

1 7 7 8 .

Capt. Smyth, the author of this bold and loyal song, was an officer in Simcoe's Queen's Rangers. Many of his compositions were published during the war. The present one first appeared in the Pennsylvania Ledger, as "a new song, to the old tune of Black Joke," and subsequently in a ballad sheet, under its present title.

THE REBELS.

YE brave, honest subjects, who dare to be loyal,
And have stood the brunt of every trial,
    Of hunting-shirts, and rifle-guns :
Come listen awhile, and I'll sing you a song ;
I'll show you, those Yankees are all in the wrong,
Who, with blustering look and most awkward gait,
'Gainst their lawful sovereign dare for to prate,
    With their hunting-shirts, and rifle-guns.

The arch-rebels, barefooted tatterdemalions,
In baseness exceed all other rebellions,
 With their hunting-shirts, and rifle-guns.
To rend the empire, the most infamous lies,
Their mock-patriot Congress, do always devise;
Independence, like the first of rebels, they claim,
But their plots will be damn'd in the annals of fame,
 With their hunting-shirts, and rifle-guns.

Forgetting the mercies of Great Britain's king,
Who saved their forefathers' necks from the string;
 With their hunting-shirts, and rifle-guns.
They renounce allegiance and take up their arms,
Assemble together like hornets in swarms,
So dirty their backs, and so wretched their show,
That carrion-crow follows wherever they go,
 With their hunting-shirts, and rifle-guns.

With loud peals of laughter, your sides, sirs, would crack,
To see General Convict and Colonel Shoe-black,
 With their hunting-shirts, and rifle-guns.
See cobblers and quacks, rebel priests and the like,
Pettifoggers and barbers. with sword and with pike,

All strutting, the standard of Satan beside,
And honest names using, their black deeds to hide.
   With their hunting-shirts, and rifle-guns.

This perjured banditti, now ruin this land,
And o'er its poor people claim lawless command,
   With their hunting-shirts, and rifle-guns.
Their pasteboard dollars, prove a common curse,
They don't chink like silver and gold in our purse;
With nothing their leaders have paid their debts off,
Their honor's, dishonor, and justice they scoff,
   With their hunting-shirts, and rifle-guns.

For one lawful ruler, many tyrants we've got,
Who force young and old to their wars, to be shot,
   With their hunting-shirts, and rifle-guns.
Our good king, God speed him! never usèd men so,
We then could speak, act, and like freemen could go;
But committees enslave us, our Liberty's gone,
Our trade and church murder'd; our country's undone,
   By hunting-shirts, and rifle-guns.

Come take up your glasses, each true loyal heart,
And may every rebel meet his due desert,
   With his hunting-shirt, and rifle-gun.

May Congress, Conventions, those damn'd inquisitions,

Be fed with hot sulphur, from Lucifer's kitchens,

May commerce and peace again be restored,

And Americans own their true sovereign lord.

Then oblivion to shirts, and rifle-guns.[1]

God save the King.

---

[1] *Then oblivion to shirts and rifle-guns.* The uniforms and equipments of the Continental soldiers were the subject of much contempt and irony on the part of the loyalists. The companies of riflemen, from the western mountains, were generally dressed in hunting-shirts and trowsers, of fawn color or brown, adorned with a fringe.

" These from the cerulean mountains hurried down ;
*   *   *   *   *   *   *
Beneath their aim the hostile leaders fall,
For death rides swift th' unseen, unerring ball."
Humphrey's Washington.

Old England.

1778.

This satirical song, entitled, "The Halcyon Days of Old England, or the wisdom of administration demonstrated; adapted to the tune of 'Ye Medley of Mortals,'" was written in England, and published in the London Evening Post, during the early part of the year seventeen hundred and seventy-eight. It was soon copied into the papers friendly to the cause of Liberty, throughout the American colonies, and became a great favorite, both in the camp, and by the firesides of the patriots.

THE HALCYON DAYS OF OLD ENGLAND.[1]

GIVE ear to my song, I'll not tell you a story;
This is the bright era of Old England's glory!
And though some may think us in pitiful plight,
I'll swear they're mistaken, for matters go right!

      Sing tantararara, wise all, wise all,
      Sing tantararara, wise all.

Let us laugh at the cavils of weak, silly elves !
Our statesmen are wise men ! they say so themselves,
And tho' little mortals may hear it with wonder,
'Tis consummate wisdom, that causes each blunder !

They are now engaged in a glorious war !
It began about tea, about feathers and tar ;[2]
With spirit they push what they've plannèd with sense !
Forty-millions they've spent, for a tax of three pence.

The debts of the nation do grieve them so sore,
To lighten our burden, they load us the more !
They aim at th' American's cash, my dear honey !
Yet beggar this kingdom, and send them the money.

What honors we're gaining by taking their forts,
Destroying bateaux, and blocking up ports !
Burgoyne would have work'd 'em but for a mishap,
By Gates and one Arnold, he's caught in a trap !

But Howe was more cautious and prudent by far,
He sail'd with his fleet up the great Delaware ;
All summer he struggled and strove to undo 'em,
But the plague of it was, he could not get to them.

9*

Oh ! think us not cruel, because our allies
Are savagely scalping men, women and boys !
Maternal affection to this step doth move us !
The more they are scalpèd, the more they will love us !

Some folks are uneasy, and make a great pother
For the loss of one army, and half of another ;
But, sirs, next campaign by ten thousands we'll slay 'em,
If we can find soldiers, and money to pay 'em.

I've sung you a song, now I'll give you a prayer ;
May peace soon succeed to this horrible war !
Again may we live with our brethren in concord,
And the authors of mischief all hang on a strong cord.

         Sing tantararara, wise all, wise all,
         Sing tantararara, wise all.

[1] *The Halcyon days of Old England.* This ballad has been attributed to Arthur Lee, who, at the time of its appearance in England, was in France.

[2] *About feathers and tar.* The discipline of tar and feathers, that the American troops inflicted upon such disaffected persons as made themselves obnoxious to the cause of liberty, was somewhat new to the royal mind, and in England was looked upon as a most " barbarous feature in warfare." It was generally applied to the obstinate and refractory loyalists, for some petty remark or unpatriotic demonstration. The riflemen from the southern colonies were celebrated

for this peculiar discipline, and the faintest vestige of toryism, was sufficient to warrant its application, to any one who should happen to fall in their way. A body of these men were passing through one of the quiet villages in Connecticut, on their march to join Washington's army, when they met a notorious loyalist, who, among other "fine names called them damned rebels and sons of sedition." They soon took him and compelled him to walk, in advance of the company, to a wood near the town of Litchfield, a distance of over twenty miles, carrying one of his own geese all the way in his hands. On their arrival there, they applied the tar, and made him pluck the goose, after which they bestowed the feathers on him, drummed him out of the company, and obliged him to kneel and thank them for their lenity. Another instance was the case of a loyal shoemaker of New York, who having "expressed a desire in public company, and in the most insolent manner" that General Gage, then in Boston, would visit that town, to cut the throats of the "rebellious whigs, and burn their houses, declaring he would himself assist in it," was immediately taken by the people and carried to the wharf, where he was stripped, and nicely fitted with a suit of "American thickset with white trimmings," and after giving him three rounds of applause, he was permitted to retire, "which he did with some precipitation," at the same time muttering ten thousand anathemas against General Gage, as the author of his disgrace.

British Light Infantry.

1 7 7 8.

This song was published in the Royal Gazette, at New York, with the accompanying remarks: " Observing in a late paper a song written for the British Light Infantry,[1] introduced with a hint that they had not hitherto received their merited tribute from the muses, I take the liberty of making them the tender of a second musical offering, which, though never yet published, has been frequently sung and re-echoed, in loyal companies, for many months past in this city; nor will the offering, perhaps, be the less welcome, for being presented in a plain, unornamented dress, and by the hand of a loyal American refugee." The song was adapted to the tune, " Black Sloven."

BRITISH LIGHT INFANTRY.

For battle prepared in their country's just cause,
Their king to avenge and support all his laws;
As fierce as a tiger, as swift as the roe,
The British Light Infantry rush on their foe.

Though rebels unnumber'd oppose their career,
Their hearts are undaunted ; they're strangers to fear ;
No obstacles hinder ; resistless they go,
And death and destruction attend every blow.

' Cross the deep-gullied vale, up the mountain's steep side,
Through the rough foaming river's impetuous tide,
O'er the fortified redoubt, close wedged in array,
Regardless of safety they follow their prey.

The alarm of the drum and the cannon's loud roar ;
The musket's quick flash, but inflames them the more.
No dangers appal, for they fear no control,
But glory and conquest inspires every soul.

Whenever their foe stands arrang'd in their sight,
With ardor impatient they pant for the fight ;
Rout, havoc, confusion they spread through the field,
And rebellion and treason are forcèd to yield.

[1] *British Light Infantry.* The song mentioned here was published in a Philadelphia paper, but is unfit for present publication.

The Old Man's Song.

1 7 7 8.

The American women, during the revolution, excelled their nature. Europe heard, with wonder and regret, of their constancy and devotion to the cause of liberty; and their spirit and firmness has been the theme of many excellent lyrics, both in this country, and the old world. We have several French ballads, commemorating their patriotism.

PUBLIC SPIRIT OF THE WOMEN.

Though age at my elbow has taken his stand,
And Time has stretch'd o'er me his wrinkling hand;
Our patriot fair like a charm can inspire,
In three-score-and-ten, twenty's spirit and fire.

Boy, fill me a bumper! as long as I live,
The patriot fair for my toast must I give;
Here's a health to the sex of every degree,
Where sweetness and beauty with firmness agree.

No more will I babble of times that are past,
My wish is, the present for ever may last;
Already I see sulky George in despair,
Should he vanquish the men, to vanquish the fair.[1]

Of Greeks and of Romans enough has been said,
To Codrus and Brutus full tribute been paid;
O'er musty old heroes no longer I'll dream,
Living beauty and virtue enliven my theme.

Could time be roll'd backward, and age become young,
My heart swell with ardor, my arm be new strung;
Under Washington's banner I'd cheerfully fight,
Where the smiles of the fair with glory unite.

Fill a bumper again boy, and let it go round,
For the waters of youth in claret are found;
The younkers shall know, I've the courage to dare
Drink as deep as the best to the patriot fair.

¹ *To vanquish the fair.* "If they had not been rebels," said Burke, "I could have been lavish in praising women, who, reduced by the ruin of civil discord to the most horrid situations of distress and poverty, had generosity and public spirit to strip the blankets, in the freezing season, from themselves and their infants, to send to the camp, and preserve that army which had gone out to fight for their liberty. And shall Britons overlook such virtue, and will they persist in oppressing it? Shall we give them no alternative but unconditional submission? A three years' war has not terrified them, distressed as they are, from their great purpose. Let us try the power of lenity over those generous bosoms."

The following verses are taken from a manuscript diary, kept during the revolution, now in possession of the editor.

> "God bless our gentle mothers, dear,
>   Who cheer us on our way!
> God bless our loving sisters, dear,
>   Who with them at home stay.
>
> We'll fight for them, and die for them,
>   To keep them from Tory!
> We'll raise our hearts in prayer for them,
>   Wherever we may be."

Battle of the Kegs.

1 7 7 8.

Early in January, 1778, David Bushnell, the inventor of the American Torpedo, and other submarine machinery, prepared a number of "infernals," as the British termed them, and set them afloat in the Delaware River, a few miles above Philadelphia, in order to annoy the royal shipping, which at that time lay off that place. These machines were constructed of kegs, charged with powder, and so arranged as to explode on coming in contact with any thing while floating along with the tide. On their appearance, the British seamen and troops became alarmed, and, manning the shipping and wharves, discharged their small arms and cannon at every thing they could see floating in the river during the ebb tide. Upon this incident the following song was composed by Francis Hopkinson, one of the happiest writers of his time. It soon became popular with Washington's army, and is mentioned by Surgeon Thacher as follows: "Our drums and fifes afforded us a favorite music till evening, when we were delighted with the song composed by Mr. Hopkinson, 'The Battle of the Kegs,' sung in the best style by a number of gentlemen."

BATTLE OF THE KEGS.

GALLANTS attend, and hear a friend,
    Trill forth harmonious ditty,
Strange things I'll tell, which late befell,
    In Philadelphia city.

'Twas early day, as poets say,
    Just when the sun was rising,
A soldier stood, on a log of wood,
    And saw a thing surprising.

As in amaze he stood to gaze,
    The truth can't be denied, sir,
He spied a score of kegs or more,[1]
    Come floating down the tide sir.

A sailor, too, in jerkin blue,
    This strange appearance viewing,
First damn'd his eyes, in great surprise,
    Then said, " some mischief's brewing.

" These kegs, I'm told, the rebels hold,
    Packed up like pickled herring,
And they're come down, t' attack the town,
    In this new way of ferrying."

The soldier flew, the sailor too,
    And scared almost to death, sir,
Wore out their shoes to spread the news,
    And ran till out of breath, sir.

Now up and down, throughout the town,
    Most frantic scenes were acted ;
And some ran here, and others there,
    Like men almost distracted.

Some fire cried, which some denied,
    But said the earth had quakèd ;
And girls and boys, with hideous noise,
    Ran through the streets half naked.

Sir William,[2] he, snug as a flea,
    Lay all this time a snoring ;
Nor dreamed of harm, as he lay warm,
    In bed with — ——.[3]

Now in a fright, he starts upright,
    Awak'd by such a clatter;
He rubs his eyes, and boldly cries,
    " For God's sake, what's the matter?"

At his bedside, he then espied,
    Sir Erskine at command, sir,'
Upon one foot he had one boot,
    And t'other in his hand, sir.

" Arise! arise, Sir Erskine cries,
    The rebels—more's the pity—
Without a boat, are all afloat,
    And rang'd before the city.

" The motley crew, in vessels new,
    With Satan for their guide, sir,
Packed up in bags, or wooden kegs,
    Come driving down the tide, sir.

" Therefore prepare for bloody war;
    These kegs must all be routed,
Or surely we despis'd shall be,
    And British courage doubted."

The royal band, now ready stand,
　　All ranged in dread array, sir,
With stomachs stout, to see it out,
　　And make a bloody day, sir.

The cannons roar from shore to shore,
　　The small arms make a rattle;
Since wars began, I'm sure no man
　　Ere saw so strange a battle.

The rebel dales, the rebel vales,
　　With rebel trees surrounded,
The distant woods, the hills and floods,
　　With rebel echoes sounded.

The fish below swam to and fro,
　　Attack'd from every quarter;
Why sure, thought they, the devil's to pay,
　　'Mongst folks above the water.

The kegs, 'tis said, though strongly made
　　Of rebel staves and hoops,⁵ sir,
Could not oppose their powerful foes,
　　The conquering British troops, sir.

From morn till night, these men of might
    Display'd amazing courage ;
And when the sun was fairly down,
    Retir'd to sup their porridge.

An hundred men, with each a pen,
    Or more, upon my word, sir,
It is most true would be too few,
    Their valor to record, sir.

Such feats did they perform that day,
    Against those wicked kegs, sir,
That years to come, if they get home,
    They'll make their boasts and brags, sir.

---

[1] *He spied a score of kegs or more.* The following prose accounts of this affair were published in the Pennsylvania Ledger, a loyal print. "The town of Philadelphia, not being as fully acquainted with the subject of the following letter taken from a Burlington paper, as the ingenious author would have his readers believe them to be, it may be necessary to relate them the fact. At the time it happened, it was so trifling as not to be thought worthy of notice in this paper, and we do not doubt but our readers will allow this letter-writer full credit for the fertility of his invention. The case was that on the fifth of January last (1778), a barrel of an odd appearance came floating down the Delaware, opposite the town, and attracted the attention of some boys, who went in pursuit of it, and had scarcely got possession of it, when it blew up, and either killed

or injured one or more of them. So far the matter was serious, and the fellow who invented the mischief may quit his conscience of the murder or injury done the lads, as well as he can. Some days after a few others of much the same appearance, and some in the form of buoys, came floating in like manner, and a few guns were, we believe, fired at them from some of the transports lying along the wharves. Other than this no notice was taken of them, except, indeed, by our author, whose imagination, perhaps as fertile as his invention, realized to himself in the frenzy of his enthusiasm the matters he has set forth." " Extract of a letter from Philadelphia, Jan. 9, 1778.—The city has been lately entertained with a most astonishing instance of the activity, bravery, and military skill of the royal navy of Great Britain. The affair is somewhat particular and deserves your notice. Some time last week, two boys observed a keg of singular construction, floating in the river opposite to the city. They got into a small boat, and in attempting to obtain the keg, it burst with a great explosion, and blew up the unfortunate boys. On Monday last, several kegs of a like construction made their appearance. An alarm was immediately spread through the city. Various reports prevailed, filling the city and royal troops with consternation. Some reported that these kegs were filled with armed rebels, who were to issue forth in the dead of the night, as did the Grecians of old from their wooden horse at the siege of Troy, and take the city by surprise, asserting that they had seen the points of their bayonets through the bung-holes of the kegs. Others said they were charged with the most inveterate combustibles, to be kindled by secret machinery, and setting the whole Delaware in flames, were to consume all the shipping in the harbor ; whilst others asserted they were constructed by art magic, would, of themselves, ascend the wharves in the night-time, and roll all flaming through the streets of the city, destroying every thing in their way. Be this as it may, certain it is that the shipping in the harbor, and all the wharves in the city, were fully manned. The battle began, and it was surprising to behold the incessant blaze that was kept up against the enemy, the kegs. Both officers and men exhibited the most unparalleled skill and bravery on the occasion, whilst the citizens stood gazing as solemn witnesses of their prowess. From the Roebuck, and other ships of war, whole broadsides were poured into the Delaware. In short, not a wandering chip, stick, or drift log, but felt the vigor of the British arms. The action began about sunrise, and would have been completed with great success by noon, had not an old market-woman, coming down the river with provisions, unfortunately let a small keg of butter fall overboard, which, as it was then ebb tide, floated down to the scene of action. At the sight of this unexpected reinforcement of the enemy, the battle was renewed with fresh fury, and the firing was incessant till evening closed the affair. The kegs were either totally demolished, or obliged to fly, as none of them have shown their *heads* since. It is said that his Excellency Lord Howe has despatched a swift-sailing packet, with an account of this victory, to the court at London. In a word, Monday, the fifth of January, seventeen hundred and seventy-eight, must ever be distinguished in history for the memorable battle of the kegs."

[2] *Sir William he, snug as a flea.* Sir William Howe commanded the British army, which entered Philadelphia on the 27th of September, 1777.

[3] *In bed with — ———.* The wife of Joshua Loring, a refugee from Boston, made commissary of prisoners by General Howe. "The consummate cruelties practised on the American prisoners under his administration, almost exceed the ordinary powers of human invention. The conduct of the Turks, in putting all prisoners to death, is certainly much more rational and humane than that of the British army for the first three years of the American war, or till after the capture of Burgoyne."

[4] *Sir Erskine at command.* Sir William Erskine, a General in the British army. He attended the expedition against Danbury, Connecticut, in 1777.

[5] *Of rebel staves and hoops.* David Bushnell was a native of Saybrook, Connecticut. The particulars of his early life are unknown. Early in the autumn of 1776, he submitted to General Washington

a machine invented by himself, for the destruction of the British shipping then at anchor in the New York harbor. The following description of the machine, and accounts of the experiments tried with it, are taken from the journal of Surgeon Thacher. "The internal appearance of the torpedo, bears some resemblance to two upper tortoise shells, of equal size, placed in contact, leaving at that part which represents the head of the animal, a flue or opening, sufficiently capacious to contain the operator, and air to support him thirty minutes. At the bottom is placed a quantity of lead for ballast. The operator sits upright, and holds an oar for rowing forward or backward, and is furnished with a rudder. A valve at the bottom admits the water for the purpose of descending, and two brass forcing pumps serve to eject the water, when necessary for ascending. Attached to the after part of this vessel is a place above the rudder for carrying a large powder magazine. This is made of two hollow pieces of oak timber, large enough to contain one hundred and fifty pounds of powder, and is secured to the object intended to be destroyed by a screw turned by the operator. Within this magazine is an apparatus, constructed to run any proposed length of time under twelve hours. On running out, it unpinions a lock, which gives the fire to the powder. This apparatus is set in motion by casting off the magazine from the operative vessel."

Bushnell was encouraged in his plan, and Major-General Putnam, being decidedly of the opinion that his operations might be attended with the desired success, resolved to be himself a spectator of the experiment. It was determined to make an attempt on the ship Eagle, on which Admiral Lord Howe commanded. "General Putnam placed himself on the wharf to witness the result. Mr. Bushnell had instructed his brother in the management of the torpedo with perfect dexterity, but, being taken sick, a sergeant * of

---

* This was Sergeant Ezra Lee, afterwards a Captain in the Continental service. He ever had the confidence and esteem of Washington, and fought with him at Trenton and Monmouth. At Brandywine the hilt of his sword was shot away, and his hat and coat pierced with the enemy's balls. On the return of peace, he retired to his farm, and tilled the land until a short time before his

a Connecticut regiment was selected for the business. Having such instructions as time would allow, late at night, he went under the ship, and attempted to fix the wooden screw into her bottom, but struck a bar of iron, which passes from the rudder-hinge, and is spiked under the ship's quarter. Had he moved a few inches, there is no doubt he would have found wood where he might have fixed the screw, but not being well skilled in the management of the vessel, in attempting to move to another place, he lost the ship. After seeking her in vain some time, he rowed off, and rose to the surface of the water, but found daylight had advanced so far, that he dare not renew the attempt. In his return from the ship, to New York, he passed near Governor's Island, and thought he was discovered by the enemy. Being in haste to avoid the danger he feared, he cast off the magazine, as he thought it retarded his progress, and in a short time it blew up with great violence, leaving the enemy to conjecture whether the stupendous noise was produced by a bomb, a meteor, a water-spout, or an earthquake. Several other attempts were made in Hudson's River, but no one succeeded."

   " In the year 1777, Mr. Bushnell made an attempt from a whale boat against the Cerberus frigate, by drawing a machine against her side by means of a line. This machine was different from the torpedo. It was constructed with wheels, furnished with irons, sharpened at the end and projecting about an inch, in order to strike the sides of the vessel when hauling it up, thereby setting the wheels in motion, which in five minutes caused the explosion. Commodore Simmons, being on board the Cerberus, wrote an official letter to Sir Peter Parker, describing the disaster occasioned by Bushnell's attempt on his ship. 'Being at anchor to the westward of New London with a schooner he had taken, discovered about eleven o'clock at night, a line towing astern from the bows. He believed that some person had veered away by it, and immediately began to haul in. A sailor belonging to the schooner, taking it for a fishing-

death. He died at Lyme, Connecticut, on the twenty-ninth of November, 1821, aged 72.

line, laid hold of it, and drew in about fifteen fathoms. At the end of the rope a machine was fastened, too heavy for one man to pull up, and other persons of the schooner coming to his assistance, drew it on deck. While they were examining it, it exploded, blew the vessel to pieces, and set her on fire. Three men were killed, and a fourth blown into the water. On examining round the ship after this occurrence, another line was discovered, which Commodore Simmons ordered to be instantly cut away, for fear of hauling up another of the infernals.' "

The Epilogue.

1778.

The ministerial press in America embraced every opportunity to ridicule the motives of the most prominent patriots of the Revolution, and very often exceeded the bounds of truth, or even probability in their assertions. The following remarks and stanzas were published in a ballad sheet, and posted in the streets of New York and Philadelphia, during the month of October 1778, and on the twenty-fourth of the same month they appeared in the Royal Gazette. " There was lately exhibited in the city of Philadelphia, an admirable farce called *Independence*. Who the author was is not positively known, but some are of the opinion that it is the work of a certain quack doctor called Franklin. Others assert that it is the joint production of the strolling company by whom it was acted ; it is, however, generally allowed, that one Adams gave the first hint, contrived the plot and cast the parts. It appeared in the exhibition so tragi-comical, that the audience were at a loss whether to laugh or cry. They were, however, well pleased with the catastrophe, and joined heartily in the following chorus. As the renowned Voltaire somewhere relates, that a song was the cause of the French reformation, the excellent actor who performed the part of the President took upon himself the plain song." The whole production has been attributed to James Rivington, "the lying hector of the Royal Gazette," but the only evidence we have to sustain this supposition, is that it was published in his paper, which is certainly very slight.

THE EPILOGUE.[1]

Our farce is now finish'd, your sport's at an end,
But ere you depart, let the voice of a friend
By way of a chorus, the evening crown
With a song to the tune of a hey derry down,
   Derry down, down, hey derry down.

Old Shakspeare, a poet, who should not be spit on,
Altho' he was born in the island called Britain,
Hath said that mankind are all players at best,
A truth we'll admit of, for sake of the jest.

On this puny stage we've strutted our hour,
And have acted our parts to the best of our power;
That the farce hath concluded not perfectly well,
Was surely the fault of the devil in hell.

This devil, you know, out of spleen to the church,
Will oftentimes leave his best friends in the lurch,
And turn them adrift in the midst of their joy;
'Tis a difficult matter to cheat the Old Boy.

Since this is the case, we must e'en make the best
Of a game that is lost; let us turn it to jest;
We'll smile, nay, we'll laugh, we'll carouse and we'll sing,
And cheerfully drink life and health to the king.

Let Washington now from his mountains descend,
Who knows but in George he may still find a friend;
A Briton, altho' he loves bottle and wench,
Is an honester fellow than parle vous French.

Our great Independence we give to the wind,
And pray that Great Britain may once more be kind.
In this jovial song all hostility ends,
And Britons and we will for ever be friends.

Boys fill me a bumper! now join in the chorus!
There is happiness still in the prospect before us,
In this sparkling glass, all hostility ends,
And Britons and we will for ever be friends.

Good night! my good people, retire to your houses,
Fair ladies, I beg you, convince your dear spouses
That Britons and we are united in bliss,
And ratify all with a conjugal kiss.

Once more, here's a health to the king and queen!
Confusion to him, who in rancor and spleen,
Refuses to drink with an English friend,
Immutable amity to the world's end.

[1] *The Epilogue.* At the time the foregoing was written, the British held possession of Philadelphia, and the Congress held its sessions at Yorktown, in Virginia. After the evacuation of the city by Howe's army, June 18, 1778, the Congress resumed its sittings there.

To Washington.

FROM THE BRITISH LIGHT INFANTRY.

1778.

GREAT Washington, thou mighty son of Mars,
Thou thund'ring hero of the rebel wars!
Accept our thanks for all thy favors past;
Our special thanks await thee for the last.

Thy proclamation, timely to command
The cattle to be fatten'd round the land,
Bespeaks thy generosity, and shows
A charity that reaches to thy foes!

And was this order issued for our sakes,
To treat us with roast beef and savory steaks?
Or was it for thy rebel train intended?
Give 'em the hides, and let their shoes be mended;

Tho' shoes are what they seldom wear of late;
'Twould load their nimble feet with too much weight!
And for the beef—there needs no puffs about it;
In short, they must content themselves without it.

We, to reward you for your care and pains,
Will visit soon your crowded stalls and plains;
And for your pamper'd cattle write, at large,
With bloody bayonets, a full discharge.

We know that we light bobs are tough and hardy,
And at a push you'll never find us tardy,
We have a stomach both for beef and battle;
So, honest whigs, once more, feed well your cattle.

Obey your chief's command, and then, 'tis plain,
We cannot want for beef the next campaign!
And if we want for fighting, be it known,
The fault, good neighbors, shall be your own!

10*

Affair of Honor.

1778.

The author of this humorous ballad is unknown. It was written at Charleston, South Carolina, a short time after the event it commemorates, and published in the ministerial issues and broadsides, as " an authentic account of the affair of honor between General Robert Howe[1] and Lieutenant-Governor Christopher Gadsden,[2] and too good a story to be told in simple prose."

AFFAIR OF HONOR.

It was on Mr. Peroy's land,
    At squire Rugeley's corner,
Great H. and G. met sword in hand,
    Upon a point of honor.

G. went before with Colonel E.,
   Together in a carriage;
On horseback followed H. and P.,
   As if to steal a marriage.

On chosen ground they now alight,
   For battle duly harness'd,
A shady place and out of sight,
   It show'd they were in earnest.

They met, and in the usual way
   With hat in hand saluted,
Which was, no doubt, to show how they
   Like gentlemen disputed.

And then they both together made
   This honest declaration,
That they came there, by honor led,
   But not by inclination.

That if they fought 'twas not because
   Of rancor, spite or passion,
But only to obey the laws
   Of custom and the fashion.

The pistols then, before their eyes,
    Were fairly prim'd and loaded!
H. wished, and so did G. likewise,
    The custom was exploded!

But as they now had gone so far
    In such a bloody business,
For action straight they both prepare
    With—mutual forgiveness.

But lest their courage should exceed
    The bounds of moderation,
Between the seconds 'twas agreed
    To fix them each a station.

The distance stepp'd by Colonel P.[3]
    Was only eight short paces;
" Now, gentlemen," says Colonel E.,[4]
    " Be sure to keep your places."

Quoth H. to G.—" Sir, please to fire!"
    Quoth G.—" No, pray begin, sir;"
And truly one must needs admire
    The temper they were in, sir.

" We'll fire both at once," said he,
　　And so they both presented;
No answer was returned by G.,
　　But silence, sir, consented.

They paus'd awhile, these gallant foes,
　　By turns politely grinning,
Till after many cons and pros,
　　H. made a brisk beginning.

He missed his mark, but not his aim,
　　The shot was well directed;
It sav'd them both from hurt and shame,
　　What more could be expected?

Then G. to show he meant no harm,
　　But hated jars and jangles,
His pistol fired across his arm,
　　From H. almost at angles.

H. now was called upon by G.,
　　To fire another shot, sir;
He smiled, and " After this," quoth he,
　　" No, truly, I cannot, sir."

Such honor did they both display,
 They highly were commended ;
And thus in short, this gallant fray
 Without mischance was ended.

No fresh dispute, we may suppose,
 Will e'er by them be started,
For now the chiefs, no longer foes,
 Shook hands, and so they parted.

[1] General Robert Howe was born at Brunswick, North Carolina, in 1734. The exact date of his birth is unknown. He was one of the earliest and boldest patriots of the South. For his gallantry during the early part of the Revolution, Congress appointed him a Brigadier-General, and ordered him to Virginia. In 1778 he was assigned to the command of the southern troops. After the unsuccessful expedition against Florida, and the defeat at Savannah, his conduct was severely, though unjustly, censured. Among others, Gadsden declaimed against him, and refusing to retract, a duel ensued, in which the only injury done was a slight scratch made upon Gadsden's cheek by the ball from Howe's weapon.

[2] Christopher Gadsden was a native of Charleston, South Carolina, where he was born in 1724. He was a member of the Congress of 1765, and also of that which met in 1774. After the capitulation of Charleston, 1780, Gadsden was sent to St. Augustine, by order of Cornwallis, and there confined in the castle nearly a year. In later life he was chosen Lieutenant-Governor, and in 1782 elected Governor, but declined on account of his age. He died in 1805.

[3] *Colonel P.*, afterwards General Charles Cotesworth Pinckney, was Howe's second in this affair.

[4] *Colonel E.* Bernard Elliot was Gadsden's second.

𝔜𝔞𝔫𝔨𝔢𝔢 𝔇𝔬𝔬𝔳𝔩𝔢'𝔰 𝔈𝔵𝔭𝔢𝔡𝔦𝔱𝔦𝔬𝔫

TO RHODE ISLAND.

1778.

This humorous ballad commemorates the attempt made upon Rhode Island, by the combined forces of Count D'Estaing, with the French fleet, and General Sullivan, in command of the American forces, during the month of August, 1778.

EXPEDITION TO RHODE ISLAND.

FROM Lewis, Monsieur Gerard came,[1]
　　To Congress in this town, sir,
They bow'd to him, and he to them,
　　And then they all sat down, sir.

Begar, said Monsieur, one grand coup,
  You shall bientot behold, sir;
This was believ'd as gospel true,
  And Jonathan felt bold, sir.

So Yankee Doodle did forget
  The sound of British drum, sir,
How oft it made him quake and sweat,
  In spite of Yankee rum, sir.

He took his wallet on his back,
  His rifle on his shoulder,
And veow'd Rhode Island to attack,
  Before he was much older.

In dread array their tatter'd crew,
  Advanc'd with colors spread, sir,
Their fifes played Yankee doodle, doo,
  King Hancock at their head, sir.[2]

What numbers bravely cross'd the seas,
  I cannot well determine,
A swarm of rebels and of fleas,
  And every other vermin.

Their mighty hearts might shrink they tho't,
    For all flesh only grass is,
A plenteous store they therefore brought,
    Of whiskey and molasses.

They swore they'd make bold Pigot squeak,[3]
    So did their good ally, sir,
And take him pris'ner in a week,
    But that was all my eye, sir.

As Jonathan so much desir'd
    To shine in martial story,
D'Estaing with politesse retir'd,[4]
    To leave him all the glory.

He left him what was better yet,
    At least it was more use, sir,
He left him for a quick retreat,
    A very good excuse, sir.

To stay, unless he rul'd the sea,
    He thought would not be right, sir,
And Continental troops, said he,
    On islands should not fight, sir.

Another cause with these combin'd,
 To throw him in the dumps, sir,
For Clinton's name alarmed his mind,[5]
 And made him stir his stumps, sir.

[1] *Monsieur Gerard came.* M. Gerard was the first ambassador from any nation to the United States. The following minute account of his reception by the Continental Congress, at Philadelphia, appeared in the papers of that period. " On Thursday, the sixth of August, 1778, the day appointed by the Congress for the reception of the minister, Richard Henry Lee, delegate from Virginia, and Samuel Adams, delegate from Massachusetts Bay, waited upon his Excellency, in a coach and six, provided by Congress, at his house. In a few minutes, the minister and the two delegates entered the coach, Mr. Lee placing himself at the minister's left hand on the back seat; Mr. Adams occupying the front seat. The minister's chariot being behind received his secretary. On the arrival of the carriages at the State House, the two members of Congress, placing themselves at the minister's left hand, a little before one o'clock, introduced him to his chair in the Congress Chamber; the President and Congress sitting. The chair was placed fronting the President. The minister being seated, he gave his credentials into the hands of his secretary, who advanced and delivered them to the President. The secretary of Congress then read and translated them, after which Mr. Lee announced the minister to the President and Congress. At this time, the President, the Congress, and the minister rose together. He bowed to the President and Congress, and they bowed to him, whereupon the whole seated themselves. In a moment, the minister rose and made a speech to the Congress, they sitting. The speech being finished, the minister sat down, and giving a copy of his speech to his secretary, he presented it to the President. The President and Congress then rose, and the President pronounced the answer to the speech, the minister standing.

The answer being ended, the whole were again seated, and the President giving a copy of the answer to the secretary of Congress, he presented it to the minister, The President, the Congress, and the minister then rose together. The minister bowed to the President, who returned the salute, and then to the Congress, who also bowed in return. And the minister having again bowed to the President, and received his bow, he withdrew, and was attended home in the same manner in which he had been conducted to the audience."

" Thus has a new and noble sight been exhibited in this new world. The Representatives of the United States of America, solemnly giving public audience to a minister plenipotentiary from the most powerful prince in Europe. Four years ago, such an event, at so near a day, was not in the view even of imagination. But it is the Almighty who raiseth up. He hath stationed America among the powers of the earth, and clothed her in robes of sovereignty."

Rivington, in the Royal Gazette of the eleventh of November, 1778, says : " A correspondent observes, that after all the pageantry and parade exhibited last summer at Philadelphia, with Monsieur Gerard, he is assured by recent accounts from thence, that, instead of an ambassador from the court of Versailles, he proves in reality nothing more than an agent from the *Fermiers Generaux* for the collection of an immense heavy debt, due to them from the rebel chiefs." Rivington concludes with the remark that Gerard is "*a driver, a mere tobacco-droger he.*"

[2] *King Hancock at their head.* John Hancock took the command of the second line of Massachusetts militia, in this movement. The advance of the American army was commanded by Colonel Livingston, the right wing by General Greene, and the left by the Marquis de la Fayette.

[3] *Bold Pigot.* Sir Robert Pigot commanded the British forces in Rhode Island.

[4] *D'Estaing with politesse retir'd.* Count D'Estaing was censured very severely for the conduct of the French fleet in this expedition.

On the day after he arrived at Newport, Lord Howe, with the British fleet, came in sight. D'Estaing went out to meet him, and after a sharp conflict, with some injury to the shipping of both sides, they separated. The British fleet went to New York, and the French returned to Newport. D'Estaing thought it necessary to go to Boston with his fleet to repair, and two days after set sail, notwithstanding the earnest protestations of the officers of the American land forces, who had been dispatched from the main army to assist in the expedition. Under these circumstances, the militia, who had volunteered with great eagerness to co-operate with their new allies, went home disgusted and disheartened, and General Sullivan ordered a retreat. So the expedition failed.

[5] *Clinton's name alarmed his mind.* Sir Henry Clinton did not arrive in the neighborhood of Rhode Island until some time after D'Estaing had left it.

This song was written in Philadelphia, but the author is unknown. Rivington published it in the Royal Gazette, at New York, on the third of October, 1778, without comment. It also appeared in the English newspapers, during the early part of the year following.

𝕬 𝕱able.

1 7 7 8.

Rivington first published this production, in the Royal Gazette, as "A fable addressed to the Americans, upon their treaty with France." It afterwards appeared as "A fable, in the way of a song, for the rebels," over the signature of D. M.[1] The last version dif_fers slightly from the original.

A FABLE.

REJOICE, Americans, rejoice !
Praise ye the Lord with heart and voice !
The treaty's signed with faithful France,
And now, like Frenchmen, sing and dance !

But when your joy gives way to reason,
And friendly hints are not deem'd treason,
Let me, as well as I am able,
Present your Congress with a fable.

Tired out with happiness, the frogs
Sedition croak'd through all their bogs;
And thus to Jove the restless race,
Made out their melancholy case.

" Fam'd, as we are, for faith and prayer,
    We merit sure peculiar care;
    But can we think great good was meant us,
    When logs for Governors were sent us?

" Which numbers crush'd they fell upon,
    And caus'd great fear,—till one by one,
    As courage came, we boldly fac'd 'em,
    Then leap'd upon 'em, and disgrac'd 'em!

" Great Jove," they croak'd, " no longer fool us,
    None but ourselves are fit to rule us;
    We are too large, too free a nation,
    To be encumber'd with taxation!

" We pray for peace, but wish confusion,
    Then right or wrong, a—revolution!
    Our hearts can never bend t' obey;
    Therefore no king—and more we'll pray."

Jove smiled, and to their fate resign'd
The restless, thankless, rebel kind;
Left to themselves, they went to work,
First signed a treaty with king Stork.

He swore that they, with his alliance,
To all the world might bid defiance;
Of lawful rule there was an end on't,
And frogs were henceforth—independent.

At which the croakers, one and all,
Proclaim'd a feast, and festival!
But joy to-day brings grief to-morrow;
Their feasting o'er, now enter sorrow!

The Stork grew hungry, long'd for fish;
The monarch could not have his wish;
In rage he to the marshes flies,
And makes a meal of his allies.

Then grew so fond of well-fed frogs,
He made a larder of the bogs!
Say, Yankees, don't you feel compunction,
At your unnatural, rash conjunction?

Can love for you in him take root,
Who's Catholic, and absolute ?
I'll tell these croakers how he'll treat 'em ;
Frenchmen, like storks, love frogs—to eat 'em.

---

[1] *D. M.* It has been suggested that David Matthews, Mayor of the city of New York, during the Revolution, was the writer of this song. D. M. is the only proof we have that such is the case.

Chester.

1778.

William Billings, the author of the subjoined hymn, was born in Boston, Massachusetts, on the seventh of October, 1746. He is more celebrated, as the earliest native writer of music in America, than by his verses. He was zealous in the cause of liberty, and the patriotic ardor which pervaded his works, made them very popular with the colonists. The New England soldiers, who, during the war, were stationed in the Southern States, had many of his tunes by heart, and amused themselves by singing them in camp, to the delight of all who hear them.

A HYMN.

LET tyrants shake their iron rod,
    And slavery clank her galling chains ;
We fear them not ; we trust in God—
    New England's God for ever reigns.
    11

Howe and Burgoyne, and Clinton, too,
   With Prescott and Cornwallis join'd;
Together plot our overthrow,
   In one infernal league combin'd.

When God inspir'd us for the fight,
   Their ranks were broke, their lines were forc'd;
Their ships were shatter'd in our sight,
   Or swiftly driven from our coast.

The foe comes on with haughty stride;
   Our troops advance with martial noise;
Their veterans flee before our youth,
   And generals yield to beardless boys.

What grateful offering shall we bring?
   What shall we render to the Lord?
Loud hallelujahs let us sing,
   And praise his name on every chord.

---

[1] *This hymn* was published in "Billings' Singing Master's Assistant," a collection of church music in general use in New England, during the Revolution. In the introduction to this work, Billings says, "Dame Gamut's sons have a strong propensity to mirth and cheerfulness, always delighting to frequent weddings and con-

certs, and some of them seem to be greatly pleased in warlike achievements, and though they carry no instruments of death or destruction, yet they are so extremely animating* that they can cause even cowards to fight, and pusillanimity to perform wonders."

The music and words of another piece in the " Singing Master's Assistant," composed by Billings was entitled

RETROSPECT.

An Anthem from sundry scriptures.

" Was not the day, was not the day,
Was not the day dark, and gloomy.
The enemy said, "let us draw a line,
Even from York to Canada."
   But praised be the Lord !
   But praised be the Lord !
The snare is broken, and we are escaped !
   But praised be the Lord !
   But blessed be the Lord !
The snare is broken, and we are escaped !
   Hark, hark, hear the adjuration,
Cursed be the man that keepeth back his sword !
   Oh ! dismal ! oh ! horrible ! oh ! dismal.
   My bowels ! my bowels !
   I am pained at my very heart !
   My heart maketh a noise within me,
For thou hast heard, oh my soul ! the alarm of war."

Billings died at Boston, September 26, 1800, aged fifty-four.

* By this is understood the fife and drum, and other martial instruments of music. *Note by the author of the hymn.*

𝔄 Song.

1778.

"Lord North's Recantation" was written by "a gentlemen of Chester," England, and first appeared in the London Evening Post. The appendix to the "Political Duenna" contains it, as do many of the newspapers published in 1779.

LORD NORTH'S RECANTATION.

When North first began,
With his taxation plan,
The Colonies all to supplant;
To Britain's true cause,
And her liberty, laws,
O, how did he scorn to recant.

Oh! how did he boast,
Of his pow'r and his host,

Alternately swagger and cant;
    Of freedom so dear,
    Not a word would he hear,
Nor believe he'd be forc'd to recant.

    That freedom he swore,
    They ne'er should have more,
Their money to give and to grant ;
    Whene'er they address'd,
    What disdain he express'd,
Not thinking they'd make him recant.

    He armies sent o'er
    To America's shore,
New government there to transplant;
    But every campaign
    Prov'd his force to be vain,
Yet still he refus'd to recant.

    But with all their bombast,
    They were so beat at last,
As to silence his impious rant ;
    Who for want of success,
    Could at last do no less,
Than draw in his horns, and recant.

With his brother Burgoyne,
He's forc'd now to join,
And a treaty of peace for to want;
Says he ne'er will fight,
But will give up his right
To taxation, and freely recant.

With the great General Howe,
He'd be very glad now,
He ne'er had engag'd in the jaunt;
And ev'ry proud Scot,
In the devilish plot,
With his lordship, are forc'd to recant.

Old England alas!
They have brought to such pass,
Too late are proposals extant;
America's lost,
Our glory at most
Is only that—tyrants recant.

A Prophecy.

1779.

THE OLD YEAR AND THE NEW.

WHAT though last year be past and gone,
  Why should we grieve or mourn about it?
As good a year is now begun,
  And better too, let no one doubt it.
        'Tis New-Year's morn; why should we part!
          Why not enjoy what heaven has sent us?
        Let wine expand the social heart,
          Let friends, and mirth, and wine content us.

War's rude alarms disturb'd last year;
  Our country bled and wept around us;
But this each honest heart shall cheer,
  And peace and plenty shall surround us.

Last year king Congo, through the land,
   Display'd his thirteen stripes to fright us ;
But George's power, in Clinton's hand,
   In this new year shall surely right us.

Last year saw many honest men,
   Torn from each dear and sweet connection,
But this shall see them home again,
   And happy in their king's protection.

Last year vain Frenchmen brav'd our coasts,
   And baffled Howe, and scap'd from Byron ;
But this shall bring their vanquish'd hosts,
   To crouch beneath the British Lion.

Last year rebellion proudly stood,
   Elate, in her meridian glory ;
But this shall quench her pride in blood ;
   George will avenge each martyr'd tory.

Then bring us wine, full bumpers bring ;
   Hail this new year in joyful chorus ;
God bless great George, our gracious king,
   And crush rebellion down before us.

A Soliloquy.

1779.

These verses were composed by Philip Freneau, a native of the city of New York. He was born on the second of January, 1752, and died December 18, 1832. He is celebrated as the most popular poet of the revolution. The greater part of his productions do not come under the class of songs or ballads. This specimen of his writings was first published in the United States Magazine, and afterwards, with some alterations and improvements, to suit the more mature judgment of the poet; it appeared in the various editions of his poems.

GEORGE THE THIRD'S SOLILOQUY.

Oh! blast this Congress, blast each upstart State,
On whose commands ten thousand warriors wait;
From various climes that dire assembly came,
True to their trust, yet hostile to my fame.
'Tis these, ah! these have ruin'd half my sway,
Disgrac'd my arms, and lead my realm astray.

France aids them now; I play a desperate game,
And sunburnt Spain they say will do the same;
My armies vanquish'd, and my heroes fled,
My people murmuring, and my commerce dead.
My shatter'd navy, pelted, bruis'd, and clubb'd,
By Dutchmen bullied, and by Frenchmen drubb'd.

My name abhorr'd, my nation in disgrace,
What should I do in such a mournful case?
My hopes and joys are vanish'd, with my coin,
My ruined army, and my lost Burgoyne!
What shall I do, confess my labors vain,
Or whet my tusks, and to the charge again?

But where's my force, my choicest troops are fled,
Some thousands crippled, and a myriad dead;
If I were owned the stoutest of mankind,
And hell with all her rage inspired my mind;
Could I at once with France and Spain contend,
And fight the rebels on the world's green end?

Yet rogues and savage tribes I must employ,
And what I cannot conquer, will destroy.

Is there a robber close in Newgate hemm'd?
Is there a cut-throat fetter'd and condemn'd?
Haste, loyal slaves, to George's standard come,
Attend his lectures when you hear the drum.

Your chains I break, for better days prepare,
Come out, my friends, from prison and from care;
Far to the west I plan your desperate way,
There, 'tis no sin, to ravage, burn, and slay;
There, without fear, your bloody trade pursue,
And show mankind what British rage can do.

Ye daring hosts that crowd Columbia's shore,
Tremble, ye traitors! and exult no more;
Flames I will hurl with an unceasing hand,
Till fires eternal blaze throughout your land;
And every dome and every town expires,
And traitors perish in the unfeeling fires.

But hold—though this be all my soul's desire,
Will my own towns be proof to rebel fire?
If in revenge my raging foes should come
And burn my London—it would strike me dumb
To see my children and my queen in tears,
And these tall piles come tumbling round my ears.

Curs'd be the day when first I saw the sun,
Curs'd be the hour when I this war begun;
The fiends of darkness then inspir'd my mind,
And powers unfriendly to the human kind;
My future years I consecrate to woe,
For this great loss my soul in tears shall flow.

To wasting grief and sullen rage a prey,
To Scotland's utmost verge I take my way;
With nature's storms eternal concert keep,
And while her billows rage as fiercely weep;
Oh! let the earth my rugged fate bemoan,
And give at least one sympathizing groan.

A Song.

1779.

These verses were published in the Royal Gazette, in March, 1779, as "A Song, written by a refugee on reading the King's speech, and sung at the Refugee Club, in the city of New York, to the tune "Hearts of Oak."

A SONG.

HERE's a bumper, brave boys, to the health of our king,
Long may he live, and long may we sing,
In praise of a monarch who boldly defends
The laws of the realm, and the cause of his friends.
 Then cheer up, my lads, we have nothing to fear,
   While we remain steady,
   And always keep ready,
 To add to the trophies of this happy year.

The Congress did boast of their mighty ally,
But George does both France and the Congress defy;
And when Britons unite, there's no force can withstand
Their fleets and their armies, by sea and on land.

Thus supported, our cause we will ever maintain,
And all treaties with rebels will ever disdain;
Till reduc'd by our arms, they are forc'd to confess,
While ruled by Great Britain they ne'er knew distress.

Then let us, my boys, Britain's right e'er defend,
Who regards not her rights, we esteem not our friend;
Then, brave boys, we both France and the Congress defy,
And we'll fight for Great Britain and George till we die.
    Then cheer up, my lads, we have nothing to fear,
        While we remain steady,
        And always keep ready,
    To add to the trophies of this happy year.

The Present Age.

1779.

The author of these sprightly verses is not known. In the
" New Hampshire Gazette " they appear, with the following note
to the printer : "By inserting this in your next paper, you will
oblige one of your country subscribers." We do not know of their
being printed elsewhere.

THE PRESENT AGE.

OF all the ages ever known,
　　The present is the oddest;
For all the men are honest grown,
　　And all the women modest.

Nor lawyers now are fond of fees,
　　Nor clergy of their dues;
No idle people now one sees,
　　At church no empty pews.

No courtiers now their friends deceive
    With promises of favor ;
For what they made 'em once believe,
    Is done and done for ever.

Our nobles—Heaven defend us all !
    I'll nothing say about 'em ;
For they are great and I'm but small,
    So muse, jog on without 'em.

Our gentry are a virtuous race,
    Despising earthly treasures ;
Fond of true honor's noble chase,
    And quite averse to pleasures.

The ladies dress so plain indeed,
    You'd think 'em Quakers all,
Witness the wool packs on their heads,
    So comely and so small.

No tradesman now forsakes his shop,
    For politics or news ;
Or takes his dealer at a hop,
    Through interested views.

No soaking sot forsakes his spouse,
    For mugs of mantling nappy;
Nor taverns tempt him from his house,
    Where all are pleas'd and happy.

Our frugal taste the State secures,
    Whence then can woes begin?
For luxury's turn'd out of doors,
    And prudence taken in.

From hence proceeds th' abundant flow,
    Of plenty through the land;
Where all provisions all men know,
    Are cheap on ev'ry hand.

No pleasure-chaises fill the streets,
    Nor crowd the roads on Sunday;
So horses ambling thro' the week,
    Obtain a respite one day.

All gaming, tricking, swearing, lying,
    Is grown quite out of fashion;
For modern youth's so self-denying,
    It flies all lawless passion.

Happy the nation thus endow'd!
　　So void of wants and crimes;
Where all are rich and none are proud,
　　Oh! these are glorious times.

Your characters (with wondering stare
　　Cries Tom) are mighty high, sir;
But pray forgive me, if I swear,
　　I think they're all a lie, sir.

Ha! think you so, my honest clown?
　　Then take another light on't;
Just turn the picture upside down,
　　I fear you'll see the right on't.

Sir Henry Clinton's

INVITATION TO THE REFUGEES.

1 7 7 9.

" Sir Harry's Invitation" was written by Philip Freneau.   We
have it in a ballad sheet, dated 1779.

THE INVITATION.

COME, gentlemen tories, firm, loyal, and true,
Here are axes and shovels, and something to do !
   For the sake of our King,
   Come labor and sing.
You left all you had for his honor and glory,
And he will remember the suffering tory.
   We have, it is true,
   Some small work to do ;

But here's for your pay, twelve coppers a day,
And never regard what the rebels may say,
But throw off your jerkins and labor away.

To raise up the rampart, and pile up the wall,
To pull down old houses, and dig the canal,
   To build and destroy,
   Be this your employ,
In the day-time to work at our fortifications,
And steal in the night from the rebels your rations.
   The king wants your aid,
   Not empty parade ;
Advance to your places, ye men of long faces,
Nor ponder too much on your former disgraces,
This year, I presume, will quite alter your cases.

Attend at the call of the fifer and drummer,
The French and the rebels are coming next summer,
   And the forts we must build
   Though tories are killed.
Take courage, my jockies, and work for your king,
For if you are taken, no doubt you will swing.
   If York we can hold,
   I'll have you enroll'd ;

And after you're dead, your names shall be read,
As who for their monarch both labor'd and bled,
And ventur'd their necks for their beef and their
bread.

'Tis an honor to serve the bravest of nations,
And be left to be hang'd in their capitulations.
Then scour up your mortars,
And stand to your quarters,
'Tis nonsense for tories in battle to run,
They never need fear sword, halberd, or gun;
Their hearts should not fail 'em,
No balls will assail 'em;
Forget your disgraces, and shorten your faces,
For 'tis true as the gospel, believe it or not,
Who are born to be hang'd, will never be shot.

A New Ballad.

1779.

This loyal song appeared originally in England. Rivington published it in the Royal Gazette, in November, 1779, and afterwards on a ballad sheet, with the chorus, "Derry Down."

A NEW BALLAD.

Rouse, Britons! at length,
And put forth your strength,
Perfidious France to resist,
Ten Frenchmen will fly,
To shun a black eye,
If an Englishman doubles his fist.
Derry down, down, hey derry down.

But if they feel stout,
Why let them turn out,

With their maws stuff'd with frogs, soups, and
    jellies;
      Brave Hardy's sea thunder,
      Shall strike them with wonder,
And make the frogs leap in their bellies!

      For their Dons and their ships,
      We care not three skips
Of a flea—and their threats turn into jest, O!
      We'll bang their bare ribs,
      For the infamous fibs,
Cramm'd into their fine manifesto.

      Our brethren so frantic,
      Across the Atlantic,
Who quit their old friends in a huff;
      In spite of their airs,
      Are at their last prayers,
And of fighting have had quantum suff.

      Then if powers at a distance,
      Should offer assistance,

Say boldly, " we want none, we thank ye,"
　　　Old England's a match,[1]
　　　And more for old scratch,
A Frenchman, a Spaniard, a Yankee !
　　　Derry down, down, hey derry down.

---

[1] *Old England's a match.* The following extempore appeared, a
short time after this song was published, in America.

> Choctaws, Chickasaws, and Catawbas,
> 　　Are all engaged to fight us;
> Keep off you Mynheers with your yaws,
> 　　And England's gun shall right us.
>
> We don't mind Monsieur's copper lace,
> 　　Nor solemn Don in cloak ;
> Once let us meet them face to face,
> 　　And fighting is no joke.
>
> Three cheers for England's weal we give,
> 　　And pour the broadside in ;
> The wretch that is not fit to live,
> 　　To kill can be no sin.

The Etiquette.

1779.

There are various versions of this sarcastic "English ballad." The subjoined copy differs from the original, first published in the London Magazine, in 1778, in one particular only.[1] The writer of it is unknown. It is included in a collection of poems, and fugitive pieces, published in London in 1779. The numerous editions of it that appeared during the last year of the Revolution, establish the fact of its popularity.

THE ETIQUETTE.

WHAT though America doth pour
Her millions to Britannia's store,
Quoth Grenville, that won't do—for yet,
Taxation is the etiquette.

The tea destroy'd, the offer made
That all the loss should be repaid—
North asks not justice, nor the debt,
But he must have the etiquette.

He'd stop their port—annul their laws—
" Hear us," cried Franklin, " for our cause ! "
To hear th' accus'd, the senate met,
Decreed 'twas not the etiquette.

At Bunker's Hill the cause was tried,
The earth with British blood was dyed ;
Our army, though 'twas soundly beat,
We hear, bore off the etiquette.

The bond dissolv'd, the people rose,
Their rulers from themselves they chose ;
Their Congress then at naught was set—
Its name was not the etiquette.

Though 'twere to stop the tide of blood,
Their titles must not be allow'd,
(Not to the chiefs of armies met,)
One Arnold was the etiquette.

The Yankees at Long Island [2] found
That they were nearly run aground ;
Howe let them 'scape when so beset—
He will explain the etiquette.

His aide-de-camps to Britain boast
Of battles—Yankee never lost;
But they are won in the Gazette—
That saves the nation's etiquette.

Clinton his injur'd honor saw,
Swore he'd be tried by martial law,
And kick Germaine whene'er they met—
A ribbon sav'd that etiquette.

Though records speak Germaine's disgrace,
To quote them to him to his face,
(The Commons now are—*si honnète*,)
They voted not the etiquette.

Of Saratoga's dreadful plain—
An army ruin'd; why complain?
To pile their arms as they were let,
Sure they came off with etiquette!

Cries Burgoyne, "They may be reliev'd,
That army still may be retriev'd,
To see the king if I be let;"
"No, sir! 'tis not the etiquette."

God save the king ! and should he choose
His people's confidence to lose,
What matters it ? they'll not forget
To serve him still—through etiquette.

1 7 7 6 .

[1] In the original publication of this song, the first is a five line
stanza, having

" Though risk it all, and nothing get,"

after the third line.

[2] *The Yankees at Long Island.* Among other incidents of the
retreat of the Americans from Long Island, in 1776, the loyal prints
circulated the following : " From report, we hear that Mr. Washington and his dirty rebel outcasts, got a good soaking the other day,
in their flight from Long Island. They were so vigorously pursued,
by our brave fellows, that many of them took to the water like dogs,
and swam over the creek. A deserter, lately come into the royal
lines, says he saw nearly all the rebel army drying their only shirt
and trowsers on the bushes, meanwhile performing various monkey
tricks and other rebel discipline, to keep warm in their buffs. He
didn't see Mr. Washington in this new rebel armor, so we suppose
he was comfortably situated in some one of those hay lofts he has
unjustly pressed from the friends of justice, right, and a loving king."

Siege of Savannah.

1779.

Count D'Estaing, with his fleet of twenty sail, reached the coast of Georgia early in September, 1779. Soon after his arrival, a plan was concerted with General Lincoln, to make a combined attack upon Savannah. Through delay and mismanagement, the Americans and their allies were repulsed. Numerous severe and ironical ballads, commemorating the event, appeared shortly after, from which the one subjoined is selected.

ABOUT SAVANNAH.

Come let us rejoice,
With heart and with voice,
Her triumphs let loyalty show, sir,
While bumpers go round,
Re-echo the sound,
Huzza for the king and Prevost, sir.

With warlike parade,
And his Irish brigade,
His ships and his spruce Gallic host, sir,
As proud as an elf,
D'Estaing came himself,
And landed on Georgia's coast, sir.

There joining a band,
Under Lincoln's command,
Of rebels and traitors and whigs, sir,
'Gainst the town of Savannah
He planted his banner,
And then he felt wonderous big, sir.

With thund'ring of guns,
And bursting of bombs,
He thought to have frighten'd our boys, sir.
But amidst all their din,
Brave Maitland push'd in,[1]
And Moncrieffe[2] cried, " A fig for your noise," sir,

Chagrined at delay,
As he meant not to stay,

The Count form'd his troops in the morn,³ sir.
　　Van, centre, and rear
　　March'd up without fear,
Cock sure of success, by a storm, sir.

　　Though rude was the shock,
　　Unmov'd as a rock,
Stood our firm British bands to their works, sir.
　　While the brave German corps,
　　And Americans bore
Their parts as intrepid as Turks, sir.

　　Then muskets did rattle,
　　Fierce ragèd the battle,
Grape shot, it flew thicker than hail, sir.
　　The ditch fill'd with slain,
　　Blood dyed all the plain,
When rebels and French turnèd tail, sir.

　　See ! see ! how they run !
　　Lord ! what glorious fun !
How they tumble, by cannon mow'd down, sir !
　　Brains fly all around,
　　Dying screeches resound,
And mangled limbs cover the ground, sir.

There Pulaski fell,[4]
That imp of old Bell,
Who attempted to murder his king,[5] sir.
But now he is gone,
Whence he'll never return ;
But will make hell with treason to ring, sir.

To Charleston with fear,
The rebels repair ;
D'Estaing scampers back to his boats, sir,
Each blaming the other,
Each cursing his brother,
And—may they cut each other's throats, sir.

Scarce three thousand men,
The town did maintain,
'Gainst three times their number of foes, sir,
Who left on the plain,
Of wounded and slain,
Three thousand to fatten the crows, sir.

Three thousand ! no less ![6]
For the rebels confess

Some loss, as you very well know, sir.
Then let bumpers go round,
And re-echo the sound.
Huzza for the king and Prevost, sir.

[1] *Brave Maitland pushed in.* D'Estaing, before his junction with Lincoln, demanded a surrender of the town to the arms of France; when Prevost asked for twenty-four hours suspension of hostilities that he might prepare proper terms. Meanwhile Colonel Maitland, with a large body of men, marched from Beaufort and joined the royal army. Prevost, thus reinforced, determined on resistance. Colonel Maitland died during the siege, of a bilious disorder.

[2] *And Moncrieffe.* Major Moncrieffe was the engineer who planned the defences of Savannah.

[3] *The Count formed his troops in the morn.* On a report from the engineers, that a long time would be required to take possession of the town by regular approaches, it was determined to make an assault. Early on the morning of the tenth of October, nearly five thousand troops, consisting of French, Continentals and the inhabitants of Charleston, marched up to the lines, led on by D'Estaing and Lincoln. But a heavy and well-directed fire from the batteries, and a cross fire from the galleys, threw them into confusion, and a retreat was ordered after they had stood the enemy's fire for fifty-five minutes. *Ramsay.*

[4] *There Pulaski fell.* Count D'Estaing and Count Pulaski were both wounded; the latter mortally. He was struck by a small cannon ball and fell from his horse, while leading his troops. In the retreat, he was borne from the field and placed upon one of the ships in the harbor, where he died. He was buried unde. a large sycamore on St. Helen's Isle, about forty miles from Savannah.

[5] *Who attempted to murder his king.* Pulaski was a native of Poland. In 1769 he was engaged in a rebellion against Stanislaus, king of Poland. In 1771, he, with a body of chosen men, entered

12*

Warsaw for the purpose of seizing the king. They so far succeeded as to carry him without the walls of the city; but were obliged to leave him, and escape from a troop of horse that were sent to over-take them. His army was afterwards defeated, and his estates con-fiscated, when he went to Paris. In 1777 he went to America and joined the army under Washington, where he distinguished himself by his good service to the cause he had embraced.

[6] *Three thousand! no less.* The French lost in killed and wounded six hundred and thirty-seven men, and the Americans four hundred and fifty-seven. The British loss did not exceed one hundred and seventy-five.

A New Song.

1779.

This ballad commemorates the attack upon Savannah. It appeared in Rivington's Gazette, as "A new song to an old tune, written by a Yankee, and sung to the tune of Doodle doo."

A NEW SONG.

THE Frenchmen came upon the coast,
Our great allies, and they did boast,
They soon would bang the British host,
    Doodle doodle do, pa, pa, pa, pa, pa.

D'Estaing he wrote to General Lincoln,
And told him that he need not think on
Danger, but in quick step march down.
    Doodle doodle do, pa, pa, pa, pa, pa.

So Lincoln came down to Savannah,
The French and we all sung hosanna,
We soon will take them every man-a.
　　Doodle doodle do, pa, pa, pa, pa, pa.

Then Maitland came just in the nick,
Or we'd have shown them such a trick,
As would have made them very sick.
　　Doodle doodle do, pa, pa, pa, pa, pa.

But soon we found ourselves mistaken,
And were glad to save our bacon,
Rather than be killed or taken.
　　Doodle doodle do, pa, pa, pa, pa, pa.

We thought to take the enemy,
But we, alas! were forced to fly,
We may do better by and by.
　　Doodle doodle do, pa, pa, pa, pa, pa.

The French, it's true, behav'd quite civil,
Yet we wish'd them to the devil,
And hope that good may spring from evil.
　　Doodle doodle do, pa, pa, pa, pa, pa.

And now that they on board are gone,
Have left poor us here all alone,
We've nought to do but sigh and moan.
    Doodle doodle do, pa, pa, pa, pa, pa.

The enemy must keep their post,
In spite of all the Gallic host,
And Georgia we've for ever lost.
    Doodle doodle do, pa, pa, pa, pa, pa.

The Recess.

1779.

This satire first appeared at London, where it was written by " a true friend of the King and the Colonies." It was reproduced in America, in 1779, on a music sheet, adapted to the tune " Yankee Doodle."

THE RECESS.[1]

AND now our Senators are gone
    To take their leave of London,
To mourn how little they have done,
    How much they have left undone !

Heaven bless 'em in their summer seats,
    And grant their neighbors stare at
The long recounting of their feats,
    Though wond'ring much what they're at !

Bless'd be the times when men may do,
 What no one comprehendeth ;
May boast of deeds that all must rue,
 Nor judge where nonsense endeth !

One year, with half ten thousand men,
 We swallow all our foes up ;
The next, the times are turn'd, and then
 Old England's scale light goes up.

But still with courage and with glee,
 New laws we must be framing ;
With paper and with parchment, we
 The savages are taming.

We swear the transatlantic folks
 Shall all obey our orders ;
While they turn all we do to jokes,
 And cry out, " guard your borders."

Well, then, we'll go to war with France—
 Yes—no—we must—we mustn't ;
John Bull shall teach Monsieur to dance—
 But can't—and there's the curse on't.

What's to be done ?—we'll end the jar—

But how ?—Ah ! there's the devil—

'Tis easier to provoke a war

By far, than cure the evil.

We trust you'll nearer hit the point

When you shall meet next winter ;

And if you cannot set the joint,

Be sure reduce the splinter.

[1] *The Recess.* The editor of the Pennsylvania Ledger, a loyal newspaper, printed at Philadelphia, had a great antipathy to " all such faint praise." " These scurrilous verses," says he, " are calculated to do more harm to our king and country, than would the defeat of one half of our army. It is only another instance of the base, perfidious means made use of by the *quiet* leaders in the present rebellion, to subvert law and the rights of the ministry. Such moderate writers ought to have *a cord* for their moderation. God save the King ! "

Dutch Song.

1 7 7 9.

This song was published in the Pennsylvania Packet, at Philadelphia, as " A song made by a Dutch lady at the Hague, for the
sailors of the five American vessels at Amsterdam. June, 1779."

DUTCH SONG.

God save the Thirteen States !
Long rule th' United States !
God save our States !
Make us victorious ;
Happy and glorious ;
No tyrants over us ;
God save our States !

Oft did America
Foresee, with sad dismay,
    Her slav'ry near.
Oft did her grievance state,
But Britain, falsely great,
Urging her desp'rate fate,
    Turn'd a deaf ear.

Now the proud British foe
We've made, by vict'ries, know,
    Our sacred right.
Witness at Bunker's Hill,
Where godlike Warren fell,
Happy his blood to spill,
    In gallant fight.

To our fam'd Washington,
Brave Stark at Bennington,
    Glory is due.
Peace to Montgomery's shade,
Who as he fought and bled,
Drew honors round his head,
    Num'rous as true.

Look to Sar'toga's plain,
Our captures on the main,
 Moultrie's defence.
Our catalogue is long,
Of heroes yet **unsung**,
Who noble feats have done
 For independence.

The melting mother's moans,
The aged father's groans,
 Have steel'd our arms.
Ye British Whigs beware!
Your chains near formèd are,
In spite of Richmond's care
 To sound alarms.

Come join your hands to ours;
No royal blocks, no tow'rs;
 God save us all!
Thus in our country's cause,
And to support our laws;
Our swords shall never pause
 At Freedom's call.

We'll fear no tyrant's nod,
Nor stern oppression's rod,
 Till Time's no more.
Thus Liberty, when driv'n
From Europe's states, is giv'n
A safe retreat and hav'n,
 On our free shore.

O, Lord ! thy gifts in store,
We pray on Congress pour,
 To guide our States.
May union bless our land,
While we, with heart and hand,
Our mutual rights defend,
 God save our States !

God save the Thirteen States !
Long watch the prosp'rous fates
 Over our States !
Make us victorious ;
Happy and glorious ;
No tyrants over us ;
 God save our States !

Volunteer Boys.

1780.

This is one of the best convivial songs produced during the war. Its authorship has been attributed to Henry Archer,[1] a native of England, who emigrated to America in 1778, and embraced the cause of the Colonists.

VOLUNTEER BOYS.

HENCE with the lover who sighs o'er his wine,
　　Cloes and Phillises toasting,
Hence with the slave who will whimper and whine,
　　Of ardor and constancy boasting.
　　　　Hence with love's joys,
　　　　Follies and noise,
The toast that I give is the Volunteer Boys.

Nobles and beauties and such common toasts,
　　Those who admire may drink, sir;
Fill up the glass to the volunteer hosts,
　　Who never from danger will shrink, sir.
　　　　Let mirth appear,
　　　　Every heart cheer,
The toast that I give is the brave volunteer.

Here's to the squire who goes to parade
　　Here's to the citizen soldier;
Here's to the merchant who fights for his trade,
　　Whom danger increasing makes bolder.
　　　　Let mirth appear,
　　　　Union is here,
The toast that I give is the brave volunteer.

Here's to the lawyer, who, leaving the bar,
　　Hastens where honor doth lead, sir,
Changing the gown for the ensigns of war,
　　The cause of his country to plead, sir.
　　　　Freedom appears,
　　　　Every heart cheers,
And calls for the health of the law volunteers.

Here's to the soldier, though batter'd in wars,
    And safe to his farm-house retir'd;
When called by his country, ne'er thinks of his scars,
    With ardor to join us inspir'd.
        Bright fame appears,
        Trophies uprear,
To veteran chiefs who became volunteers.

Here's to the farmer who dares to advance
    To harvests of honor with pleasure;
Who with a slave the most skilful in France,
    A sword for his country would measure.
        Hence with cold fear,
        Heroes rise here;
The ploughman is chang'd to the stout volunteer.

Here's to the peer, first in senate and field,
    Whose actions to titles add grace, sir;
Whose spirit undaunted would never yet yield
    To a foe, to a pension or place, sir.
        Gratitude here,
        Toasts to the peer,
Who adds to his titles, " the brave volunteer."

Thus the bold bands for old Jersey's defence,

    The muse hath with rapture review'd, sir ;

With our volunteer boys, as our verses commence,

    With our volunteer boys they conclude, sir.

        Discord or noise,

        Ne'er damp our joys,

But health and success to the volunteer boys.

[1] *Henry Archer.*   " Dr. French," a nephew of the celebrated Jonathan French (minister at Andover, Mass.), now living in the town of Rockingham, Vermont, says he often heard his father say that " Henry Archer, a gentleman from England," was the author of the " Volunteer Boys."   By referring to the Pennsylvania Packet, October, 1778, the reader will find the following.   " Philadelphia— Friday last, arrived in this city, Henry Archer, Ėsq.   This young gentleman has been educated at a military school, in England, where he owned a handsome fortune, which he has lately sold, in order to embark as a volunteer in the American army."

An Appeal.

1780.

This song was transposed by a refugee, and intended for the loyalists without the lines, while D'Estaıng was in Georgia; but it was not published until some time after the French fleet had left the coast. It was adapted to the tune "The Cut-Purse," and became very popular with the friends of royalty, during the latter part of the war.

A SONG.

THE old English cause knocks at every man's door,
    And bids him stand up for religion and right;
It addresses the rich as well as the poor;
    And fair liberty, bids them, like Englishmen fight.
          And suffer no wrong,
          From a rebel throng,
Who, if they're not quelled, will enslave us ere long;
      13

Most bravely then let us our liberty prize,
Nor suffer the Congress to blind all our eyes,
    Or each rebel cut-purse, will soon give us law,
    For they are as bad as a Tyler or Straw.

From France, D'Estaing to America has come.
  The French banditti will rob our estates;
These robbers are all protected by Rome;[1]
  Consult but their annals, record but their dates,
        It's their politics
        To burn heretics,
Or poison by water that's fetch'd from the Styx.
Let Frenchified rebels, in vain then attempt
To bring our own church, or our king to contempt;
    For no rebel cut-purse shall e'er give us law,
    Should they prove as daring as Tyler or Straw.

The farces of Rome, with carrying her hosts,
  Are laugh'd at and jeer'd by the learnèd and wise,
And all her thin tinsels apparently lost,
  Her stories of relics, and sanctified lies.
        Each ignorant joke
        Believe, or you smoke,
And if we are conquer'd we receive the Pope's yoke;

But despising the counsels of Adams and Lee,
As loyal Americans, we'll die or be free.
> For no rebel cut-throat shall e'er give us law,
> Should they prove as daring as Tyler or Straw.

Let curses most vile, and anathemas roar,
> Let half-ruin'd France, to the Pope tribute pay ;
Britain's thundering cannon, shall guard safe our shore ;
> Great George shall defend us, none else we'll obey
>> Then France, join'd by Spain,
>> May labor in vain,
For soon the Havana shall be ours again.
The French then will scamper and quit every state,
And find themselves bubbled, when *morbleu* it's too
> late.
> For no Frenchman, or rebel imp of the law,
> In our old constitution can point out a flaw.

---

[1] *These robbers are all protected by Rome.* The loyal writers used
every effort to frighten the patriots into a return to their allegiance
to the king of Great Britain. Among these, they pictured the
supremacy of the Pope as a sure consequence upon the success of
the French in America, and invented many absurd stories about the
"inevitable destruction of life, liberty and property, that must ensue
if the rebel Congress should have its sway." The following appeared
in Rivington's Gazette : "The clergy and selectmen of Boston

paraded through the streets after a crucifix, and joined in a procession in praying for a departed soul out of purgatory; and for this, they gave the example of Congress, and other American leaders, on a former occasion at Philadelphia, some of whom in the height of their zeal, even went so far as to sprinkle themselves with what they call holy water."

At another time Rivington published: "On the receipt of the last manifesto from the English commissioners, one of the Congress had the resolution to make the following short speech: 'I have listened to this manifesto with great attention, and am not ashamed to acknowledge that it breathes a spirit of candor and resolution by which I am considerably influenced. No man in this august assembly will dare to express a doubt of my sincere attachment to the true interest of my country. I am convinced that the interest of America is inseparable from that of Britain, and that our alliance with France is unnatural, unprofitable, and absurd. I therefore move that this phantom of *Independence* may be given up.'

"He had hardly uttered the words before the president sent a messenger to fetch the Polish Count Pulaski, who happened to be exercising a part of his legion in the court-yard below. The Count flew to the chamber where the Congress sat, and with his sabre in an instant severed from his body the head of this honest delegate. The head was ordered by the Congress to be fixed on the top of the liberty pole of Philadelphia, as a perpetual monument of the freedom of debate in the Continental Congress of the United States of America."

Charleston.

1780.

The reduction of Charleston, South Carolina, by the British, in 1780, was the subject of numerous songs and poems. The subjoined specimen was written by an officer of the royal army, and first published in a ballad-sheet, set to the tune of the "Watery God."

A SONG ABOUT CHARLESTON.

KING HANCOCK [1] sat in regal state,
And big with pride and vainly great,
    Address'd his rebel crew,
These haughty Britons soon shall yield
The boasted honors of the field,
    While our brave sons pursue.

Six thousand fighting men or more,
Protect the Carolina shore,
 And Freedom will defend;
And stubborn Britons soon shall feel,
'Gainst Charleston, and hearts of steel,
 How vainly they contend.

But ere he spake in dread array,
To rebel foes, ill-fated day,
 The British boys appear;
Their mien with martial ardor fir'd,
And by their country's wrongs inspir'd,
 Shook Lincoln's heart with fear.

See Clinton brave, serene, and great,
For mighty deeds rever'd by fate,
 Direct the thund'ring fight,
While Mars, propitious God of war,
Looks down from his triumphal car,
 With wonder and delight.

" Clinton," he cries, " the palm is thine,
'Midst heroes thou wert born to shine,
 A great immortal name,

And Cornwallis' mighty deeds appear,
Conspicuous each revolving year,
   The pledge of future fame."

Our tars, their share of glories won,
For they among the bravest shone,
   Undaunted, firm and bold.
Whene'er engag'd, their ardor show'd
Hearts which with native valor glow'd,
   Hearts of true British mould.

[1] *King Hancock.* About the time this ballad was written, the subjoined paragraph appeared in the loyal newspapers : "John Hancock and Samuel Adams.—Fortune, in one of her highest frolics, elevated those malignant stars to the zenith of power. The baneful influence of their conjunction, in the Western political hemisphere, has produced direful effects ; but, when the lunacies of the former are separated from the villanies of the latter, the deluge of destruction that is certainly, though slowly, rolling after them, will rapidly come on, and overwhelm them and their infatuated votaries in prodigious ruin.

"John Hancock appears in public with all the pageantry and state of an Oriental prince. He rides in an elegant chariot, which was taken in a prize to the 'Civil Usage,' a pirate vessel, and by the owners presented to him. He is attended by four servants, dressed in superb livery, mounted on fine horses richly caparisoned, and escorted by fifty horsemen with drawn sabres, the one half of whom precede, and the other follow, his carriage. So, at present, figures this man, who owes his greatness to his country's ruin."

Our Women.

1780.

These lines were addressed to the females of Pennsylvania and New Jersey, " who illustrated the nobility of their sentiment and virtue of their patriotism, by generous subscriptions to the suffering soldiers of the American army." The author is unknown.

OUR WOMEN.

ALL hail! superior sex, exalted fair,
Mirrors of virtue, Heaven's peculiar care;
Form'd to enspirit and enoble man
The immortal finish of Creation's plan!

Accept the tribute of our warmest praise
The soldier's blessing and the patriot's bays!
For fame's first plaudit we no more contest
Constrain'd to own it decks the female breast.

While partial prejudice is quite disarm'd,
And e'en pale envy with encomiums charm'd,
Freedom no more shall droop her languid head,
Nor dream supine on sloth's lethargic bed.

No more sit weeping o'er the veteran band,
Those virtuous, brave protectors of her land;
Who, nobly daring, stem despotic sway,
And live the patriot wonders of the day.

For lo ! these sons her glorious work renew,
Cheer'd by such gifts, and smiles, and pray'rs from
    you !
More precious treasure in the soldier's eye
Than all the wealth Potosi's mines supply.

And now ye sister angels of each state,
Their honest bosoms glow with joy elate,
Their gallant hearts with gratitude expand
And trebly feel the bounties of your hand.

And wing'd for you their benedictions rise,
Warm from the soul and grateful to the skies !
Nor theirs alone th' historian patriots fir'd,
Shall bless the generous virtue you've inspir'd.

Invent new epithet to warm their page,
And bid you live admired from age to age;
With sweet applauses dwell on every name,
Endear your memories and embalm your fame,

And thus the future bards shall soar sublime,
And waft you glorious down the stream of time ;
The breeze of panegyric fill each sail,
And plaudits pure perfume the increasing gale.

Then freedom's ensign thus inscribed shall wave,
" The patriot females who their country save ; "
Till time's abyss absorb'd in heavenly lays,
Shall flow in your eternity of praise.

The Cow Chace.

1780.

This ballad was written by Major John Andre,[1] and first published in the Royal Gazette. It commemorates the attack of General Wayne, upon the Refugee's Block House, situated on the Hudson River, about four miles below Fort Lee, on the twenty-first of July, 1780.

THE COW CHACE.[2]

PART I.

To drive the kine one summer's morn,
　　The tanner took his way;
The calf shall rue that is unborn,
　　The jumbling of that day.

And Wayne descending steers shall know,
　　And tauntingly deride;
And call to mind in every low,
　　The tanning of his hide.

Yet Bergen cows still ruminate,
    Unconscious in the stall,
What mighty means were used to get,
    And loose them after all.

For many heroes bold and brave,
    From Newbridge and Tappan,
And those that drink Passaic's wave,
    And those who eat supaun;

And sons of distant Delaware,
    And still remoter Shannon,
And Major Lee with horses rare,
    And Proctor with his cannon.

All wond'rous proud in arms they came,
    What hero could refuse
To tread the rugged path to fame,
    Who had a pair of shoes!

At six, the host with sweating buff,
    Arrived at Freedom's pole;
When Wayne, who thought he'd time enough,
    Thus speechified the whole.

" O ye, who glory doth unite,
    Who Freedom's cause espouse ;
Whether the wing that's doom'd to fight,
    Or that to drive the cows,

" Ere yet you tempt your further way,
    Or into action come,
Hear, soldiers, what I have to say,
    And take a pint of rum.

" Intemp'rate valor then will string
    Each nervous arm the better ;
So all the land shall I O sing,
    And read the General's letter.

" Know that some paltry refugees,
    Whom I've a mind to fight ;
Are playing h—l amongst the trees
    That grow on yonder height.

" Their fort and block-houses we'll level,
    And deal a horrid slaughter ;
We'll drive the scoundrels to the devil,
    And ravish wife and daughter.

" I, under cover of attack,
    Whilst you are all at blows,
From English neighb'rhood and Nyack
    Will drive away the cows;

" For well you know the latter is
    The serious operation,
And fighting with the refugees
    Is only demonstration."

His daring words, from all the crowd,
    Such great applause did gain,
That every man declar'd aloud,
    For serious work with Wayne.

Then from the cask of rum once more,
    They took a heady gill;
When one and all, they loudly swore,
    They'd fight upon the hill.

But here the muse hath not a strain
    Befitting such great deeds;
Huzza! they cried, huzza! for Wayne,
    And shouting ————.

Part II.

Near his meridian pomp, the sun
    Had journey'd from the horizon ;
When fierce the dusky tribe mov'd on,
    Of heroes drunk as pison.

The sounds confus'd of boasting oaths,
    Re-echo'd through the wood ;
Some vow'd to sleep in dead men's clothes,
    And some to swim in blood.

At Irving's nod 'twas fine to see,
    The left prepare to fight ;
The while, the drovers, Wayne and Lee,
    Drew off upon the right.

Which Irving 'twas, fame don't relate,
    Nor can the muse assist her ;
Whether 'twas he that cocks a hat,
    Or he that gives a clyster

For greatly one was signaliz'd,
 That fought on Chestnut Hill;
And Canada immortaliz'd
 The vender of the pill.

Yet the attendance upon Proctor,
 They both might have to boast of;
For there was business for the doctor,
 And hats to be disposed of.

Let none uncandidly infer,
 That Stirling wanted spunk;
The self-made peer had sure been there,
 But that the peer was drunk.

But turn we to the Hudson's banks,
 Where stood the modest train;
With purpose firm, though slender ranks,
 Nor car'd a pin for Wayne.

For them the unrelenting hand
 Of rebel fury drove;
And tore from every genial band
 Of friendship and of love.

And some within a dungeon's gloom,
 By mock tribunals laid;
Had waited long a cruel doom
 Impending o'er each head.

Here one bewails a brother's fate,
 There one a sire demands,
Cut off, alas! before their date,
 By ignominious hands.

And silver'd grandsires here appear'd
 In deep distress serene,
Of reverent manners that declar'd
 The better days they'd seen.

Oh, curs'd rebellion, these are thine,
 Thine are these tales of woe;
Shall at thy dire insatiate shine,
 Blood never cease to flow?

And now the foe began to lead
 His forces to the attack;
Balls whistling unto balls succeed,
 And make the block-house cracl
 17

No shot could pass, if you will take
    The General's word for true;
But 'tis a d——ble mistake,
    For every shot went through.

The firmer as the rebels press'd,
    The loyal heroes stand;
Virtue had nerv'd each honest breast,
    And industry each hand.

" In valor's frenzy, Hamilton,
    Rode like a soldier big,
And secretary Harrison,
    With pen stuck in his wig."

" But lest their chieftain Washington,
    Should mourn them in the mumps,
The fate of Withrington to shun,
    They fought behind the stumps."

But ah, Thaddeus Posset, why
    Should thy poor soul elope ?
And why should Titus Hooper die,
    Ay, die—without a rope ?

Apostate Murphy, thou to whom
    Fair Shela ne'er was cruel,
In death shalt hear her mourn thy doom,
    " Och! would you die, my jewel ? "

Thee, Nathan Pumpkin, I lament,
    Of melancholy fate;
The gray goose stolen as he went,
    In his heart's blood was wet.

Now, as the fight was further fought,
    And balls began to thicken,
The fray assum'd, the generals thought,
    The color of a lickin'.

Yet undismay'd the chiefs command,
    And to redeem the day ;
Cry, Soldiers, charge ! they hear, they stand,
    They turn and run away.

PART III.

Not all delights the bloody spear,
   Or horrid din of battle ;
There are, I'm sure, who'd like to hear
   A word about the cattle.

The chief whom we beheld of late,
   Near Schralenburg haranguing,
At Yan Van Poop's unconscious sat
   Of Irving's hearty banging.

Whilst valiant Lee, with courage wild,
   Most bravely did oppose
The tears of woman and of child,
   Who begg'd he'd leave the cows.

But Wayne, of sympathizing heart,
   Requirèd a relief ;
Not all the blessings could impart
   Of battle or of beef.

For now a prey to female charms,
 His soul took more delight in
A lovely hamadryad's arms,
 Than cow-driving or fighting.

A nymph the refugees had drove
 Far from her native tree,
Just happen'd to be on the move,
 When up came Wayne and Lee.

She, in mad Anthony's fierce eye,
 The hero saw portray'd,
And all in tears she took him by
 — The bridle of his jade.

" Hear," said the nymph, " O, great commander!
 No human lamentations ;
The trees you see them cutting yonder,
 Are all my near relations.

" And I, forlorn ! implore thine aid,
 To free the sacred grove ;
So shall thy prowess be repaid
 With an immortal's love."

Now some, to prove she was a goddess,
    Said this enchanting fair
Had late retirèd from the bodies
    In all the pomp of war.

The drums and merry fifes had play'd
    To honor her retreat;
And Cunningham himself convey'd
    The lady through the street.

Great Wayne, by soft compassion sway'd,
    To no inquiry stoops,
But takes the fair afflicted maid
    Right into Yan Van Poop's.

So Roman Anthony, they say,
    Disgrac'd the imperial banner,
And for a gypsy lost a day,
    Like Anthony the tanner.

The hamadryad had but half
    Receiv'd address from Wayne,
When drums and colors, cow and calf,
    Came down the road amain.

And in a cloud of dust was seen
　　The sheep, the horse, the goat,
The gentle heifer, ass obscene,
　　The yearling and the shoat.

And pack-horses with fowls came by,
　　Befeather'd on each side ;
Like Pegasus, the horse that I
　　And other poets ride.

Sublime upon his stirrups rose
　　The mighty Lee behind,
And drove the terror-smitten cows
　　Like chaff before the wind.

But sudden see the woods above,
　　Pour down another corps,
All helter-skelter in a drove,
　　Like that I sung before.

Irving and terror in the van,
　　Came flying all abroad ;
And cannon, colors, horse, and man,
　　Ran tumbling to the road.

Still as he fled, 'twas Irving's cry,
 And his example too,
" Run on, my merry men—For why?
 The shot will not go through." [3]

As when two kennels in the street,
 Swell'd with a recent rain,
In gushing streams together meet,
 And seek the neighboring drain;

So met these dung-born tribes in one,
 As swift in their career,
And so to Newbridge they ran on—
 But all the cows got clear.

Poor Parson Caldwell, all in wonder,
 Saw the returning train,
And mourn'd to Wayne the lack of plunder
 For them to steal again.

For 'twas his right to steal the spoil, and
 To share with each commander,
As he had done at Staten Island
 With frost-bit Alexander.

In his dismay, the frantic priest,
    Began to grow prophetic;
You'd swore, to see his laboring breast,
    He'd taken an emetic.

" I view a future day," said he,
    " Brighter than this day dark is;
And you shall see what you shall see,
    Ha! ha! my pretty Marquis!

" And he shall come to Paulus Hook,
    And great achievements think on;
And make a bow and take a look,
    Like Satan over Lincoln.

" And every one around shall glory
    To see the Frenchman caper;
And pretty Susan tell the story
    In the next Chatham paper."

This solemn prophecy, of course,
    Gave all much consolation,
Except to Wayne, who lost his horse,
    Upon that great occasion.
        14

His horse that carried all his prog,
    His military speeches;
His corn-stock whiskey for his grog,
    Blue stockings and brown breeches.

And now I've clos'd my epic strain,
    I tremble as I show it,
Lest this same warrior-drover, Wayne,
    Should ever catch the poet.

[1] *John Andre.* The history of this young officer is well known All that we know of his literary efforts, is given in the following advertisement, which appeared in Rivington's Gazette a short time after he was executed. " Monody on Major Andre, by his friend and correspondent, Miss Seward ; with three letters, written by him, at eighteen years of age, to a most accomplished young lady, the object of his tenderest affection ; also a few copies of the three cantos of the Cow Chace, which makes the collection complete respecting the literary productions of this ever-valued and universally beloved young gentleman."

[2] *Cow Chace.* Three or four miles below Fort Lee, at the base of the Palisades, on Hudson River, is a little village called Bull's Ferry. Just below this village, was a block-house, occupied in the summer of 1780, by a British picket, for the protection of some wood-cutters, and the neighboring Tories. On Bergen Neck, below, was a large number of cattle and horses, within reach of the British foragers, who might go out from the fort at Paulus Hook. Washington then sent General Wayne, with some Pennsylvania and Maryland troops, to storm the work on Blockhouse Point, and to drive the cattle within the American lines. Wayne sent the cavalry, under Major Lee, to perform the latter duty, while he and three.

Pennsylvania regiments marched against the block-house with four pieces of artillery. They made a spirited attack, but their cannons were too light to be effective, and, after a skirmish, the Americans were repulsed, with a loss in killed and wounded of sixty-four men. After burning some wood-boats near, and capturing the men in charge of them, Wayne returned to camp with a large number of cattle, driven by the dragoons.—*Lossing's Field Book.*

The last canto of this epic was published on the day when Andre was captured. The original copy is still in existence, and has the following endorsement upon it, under the signature of Major Andre.

> " When the epic strain was sung,
> The poet by the neck was hung,
> And to his cost he finds too late,
> The dung-born tribe decides his fate."

[3] *The shot will not go through.* The following is a poetical note by the author of the song.

> " Five refugees ('tis true) were found,
> Stiff on the block-house floor;
> But then 'tis thought the shot went round,
> And in at the back door."

John Paulding.

1780.

The incidents connected with the capture and trial of Major Andre are well known. Many songs have been written, lamenting his unhappy fate. The one subjoined we copy from a ballad-sheet printed in 1783.

BRAVE PAULDING AND THE SPY.

Come all you brave Americans,
　And unto me give ear,
And I'll sing you a ditty
　That will your spirits cheer,
Concerning a young gentleman
　Whose age was twenty-two;
He fought for North America,
　His heart was just and true.

They took him from his dwelling,
   And they did him confine,
They cast him into prison,
   And kept him there a time.
But he with resolution
   Resolv'd not long to stay;
He set himself at liberty,
   And soon he ran away.

He with a scouting-party
   Went down to Tarrytown,
Where he met a British officer,
   A man of high renown;
Who says unto these gentlemen,
   " You're of the British cheer,
I trust that you can tell me
   If there's any danger near ? "

Then up stept this young hero,
   John Paulding was his name,
" Sir, tell us where you're going,
   And, also, whence you came ? "
" I bear the British flag, sir;
   I've a pass to go this way,

I'm on an expedition,
　　And have no time to stay."

Then round him came this company,
　　And bid him to dismount;
" Come, tell us where you're going,
　　Give us a strict account;
　For we are now resolvèd,
　　That you shall ne'er pass by."
　Upon examination
　　They found he was a spy.

He beggèd for his liberty,
　　He plead for his discharge,
　And oftentimes he told them,
　　If they'd set him at large,
" Here's all the gold and silver
　　I have laid up in store,
　But when I reach the city,
　　I'll give you ten times more."

" I want not the gold and silver
　　You have laid up in store,
　And when you get to New York,
　　You need not send us more;

But you may take your sword in hand
　　To gain your liberty
And if that you do conquer me
　　O, then you shall be free."

" The time it is improper
　　Our valor for to try,
For if we take our swords in hand,
　　Then one of us must die ;
I am a man of honor,
　　With courage true and bold,
And I fear not the man of clay,
　　Although he's cloth'd in gold."

He saw that his conspiracy
　　Would soon be brought to light ;
He begg'd for pen and paper,
　　And askèd leave to write
A line to General Arnold,
　　To let him know his fate,
And beg for his assistance ;
　　But now it was too late.

When the news it came to Arnold,
　It put him in a fret;
He walk'd the room in trouble,
　Till tears his cheek did wet;
The story soon went through the camp,
　And also through the fort;
And he callèd for the Vulture
　And sailèd for New York.

Now Arnold to New York is gone,
　A-fighting for his king,
And left poor Major Andre
　On the gallows for to swing;
When he was executed,
　He looked both meek and mild;
He look'd upon the people,
　And pleasantly he smil'd.

It mov'd each eye with pity,
　Caus'd every heart to bleed,
And every one wish'd him releas'd
　And Arnold in his stead.

He was a man of honor,
　　In Britain he was born;
To die upon the gallows
　　Most highly he did scorn.

A bumper to John Paulding!
　　Now let your voices sound,
Fill up your flowing glasses,
　　And drink his health around;
Also to those young gentlemen
　　Who bore him company;
Success to North America,
　　Ye sons of liberty!

Sergeant Champe.

1780.

The adventure of this gallant officer, commemorated in the subjoined ballad, is connected with the conspiracy of Arnold. The authorship of the song is unknown, as is the case of very many of the finest productions of the Revolutionary period. It was adapted to the air of "Barbara Allen," and sung very generally, at home and in the camp, during the last years of the Revolution.

SERGEANT CHAMPE.[1]

Come sheathe your swords! my gallant boys,
    And listen to the story,[2]
How Sergeant Champe, one gloomy night,
    Set off to catch the tory.

You see the general had got mad,
    To think his plans were thwarted,
And swore by all, both good and bad,
    That Arnold should be carted.

So unto Lee he sent a line,
    And told him all his sorrow,
And said that he must start the hunt,
    Before the coming morrow.

Lee found a sergeant in his camp,
    Made up of bone and muscle,
Who ne'er knew fear, and many a year
    With tories had a tussle.

Bold Champe, when mounted on old Rip,
    All button'd up from weather,
Sang out, " good bye ! " crack'd off his whip,
    And soon was in the heather.

He gallop'd on towards Paulus Hook,
    Improving every instant—
Until a patrol, wide awake,
    Descried him in the distance.

On coming up, the guard call'd out
    And ask'd him where he's going—
To which he answer'd with his spur,
    And left him in the mowing.

The bushes pass'd him like the wind,
     And pebbles flew asunder.
The guard was left far, far behind,
     All mix'd with mud and wonder.

Lee's troops paraded, all alive,
     Although 'twas one the morning,
And counting o'er a dozen or more,
     One sergeant is found wanting.

A little hero,[3] full of spunk,
     But not so full of judgment,
Press'd Major Lee to let him go,
     With the bravest of his reg'ment.

Lee summon'd cornet Middleton,
     Expressèd what was urgent,
And gave him orders how to go
     To catch the rambling sergeant.

Then forty troopers, more or less,
     Set off across the meader;
'Bout thirty-nine went jogging on
     A-following their leader.

At early morn, adown a hill
    They saw the sergeant sliding;
So fast he went, it was not ken't,
    Whether he's rode, or riding.

None lookèd back, but on they spurr'd,
    A-gaining every minute.
To see them go, 'twould done you good,
    You'd thought old Satan in it.

The sergeant miss'd 'em, by good luck,
    And took another tracing,
He turn'd his horse from Paulus Hook,
    Elizabethtown facing.

It was the custom of Sir Hal
    To send his galleys cruising,
And so it happenèd just then,
    That two were at Van Deusen's.

Strait unto these the sergeant went,
    And left old Rip, all standing,
A waiting for the blown cornet,
    At Squire Van Deusen's landing.

The troopers didn't gallop home,
    But rested from their labors ;
And some 'tis said took gingerbread
    And cider from the neighbors.

'Twas just at eve the troopers reach'd
    The camp they left that morning.
Champe's empty saddle, unto Lee,
    Gave an unwelcome warning.

" If Champe has suffered, 'tis my fault;"
    So thought the generous major :
" I would not have his garment touch'd,
    For millions on a wager ! "

" The cornet told him all he knew,
    Excepting of the cider.
The troopers, all, spurr'd very well
    But Champe was the best rider ! "

And so it happen'd that brave Champe
    Unto Sir Hal deserted,
Deceiving him, and you, and me,
    And into York was flirted.

He saw base Arnold in his camp,
    Surrounded by the legion,
And told him of the recent prank
    That threw him in that region.

Then Arnold grinn'd, and rubb'd his hands,
    And e'enmost chok'd with pleasure,
Not thinking Champe was all the while
    A " taking of his measure."

" Come now," says he, " my bold soldier,
    As you're within our borders,
Let's drink our fill, old care to kill,
    To-morrow you'll have orders."

Full soon the British fleet set sail!
    Say! wasn't that a pity?
For thus it was brave Sergeant Champe
    Was taken from the city.

To southern climes the shipping flew,
    And anchored in Virginia,
When Champe escaped and join'd his friends
    Among the picininni.

Base Arnold's head, by luck, was sav'd,
     Poor Andre was gibbeted,
   Arnold's to blame for Andre's fame,
     And Andre's to be pitied.

[1] *Sergeant John Champe* was " a native of Loudon county, in Virginia, rather above the ordinary size, full of physical power, with a countenance grave and thoughtful." He enlisted in the Continental army at the age of nineteen, where he served with honor to himself and the corps to which he belonged. He was honorably discharged from service, by Gen. Washington, on the conclusion of his hazardous adventure, lest he might be taken by the enemy and hung ; and soon after retired to his home in Loudon county. In 1798 he removed to Kentucky, where he remained until the time of his death.

[2] *And listen to the story.* General Washington, on his return to the army, immediately sent for Major Lee. This officer, on repairing to head-quarters, found the general alone in his marquee busily engaged in writing. As soon as he entered, a bundle of papers was laid before him for perusal, in which he found much information tending to prove that Arnold was not alone in the conspiracy, but that among others, a major-general, whose name was not concealed, was as guilty as Arnold himself. It was for the purpose of forming a plan to ascertain the truth of these suggestions, as well as for the capture of Arnold, that Washington had summoned Lee, and the project was known to them alone. " It is my desire," said Washington, " to probe to the bottom the intelligence contained in the papers you have just read ; to seize Arnold, and by securing him, to render it possible for me to restore the amiable and unfortunate Andre to his friends. Have you, in your legion, a person capable and willing to undertake a delicate and dangerous project ? Whoever comes forward, will lay me under great personal obligations, and in behalf of the nation I will reward him." Lee suggested a ser-

geant of the cavalry as one in all respects qualified for the adventurous scheme, "being a man of tried courage and inflexible perseverance, and as likely to reject an overture coupled with ignominy as any officer in the corps." The general was delighted to find that a non-commissioned officer was capable of carrying out his views, and Lee returned to camp with his instructions to confer with Champe, as it was the design he should set off that night. After a long consultation, Champe was prevailed upon to undertake the enterprise. The instructions were read to him, and from them he prepared notes so disguised as to be understood only by himself. Arnold was upon no account to be injured, but to be allowed to escape rather than to be killed in preventing such an event. It was the desire of Washington to make a public example of him.

No time was lost. Champe immediately prepared himself and his horse for the journey, and a little before midnight, mounted to pursue his way to Paulus Hook. Within half an hour Captain Carnes, officer of the day, repaired to the quarters of Major Lee, and told him that the guard had fallen in with a dragoon, who, upon being questioned, put spurs to his horse and escaped; at the same time requesting orders for the pursuit. The major, who had assured Champe, that, in the event of his desertion being discovered before morning, he would delay the pursuit as long as possible, tried every device to accomplish it. He complained of the disturbance of his sleep, and suggested the probability of its being a countryman on his way home, or some soldier gone out on a tour of personal pleasure. Captain Carnes then returned to his quarters, paraded the troops and found one sergeant missing, of which he hastily informed Major Lee. Some delay was occasioned by these movements. Champe had been gone but an hour, when the troopers, under the command of a cornet, set off on the chase. A shower of rain had fallen soon after the sergeant's departure, which enabled the dragoons to take his trail. On they spurred, stopping occasionally during the darkness of the night, to examine the foot-prints of the fugitive's horse.* When morning broke, no longer forced to halt, they passed

* The shoes of the horses were all made in the same form; which, with a

ɔn rapidly. Ascending the summit of a hill, a few miles north of the village of Bergen, they descried Champe, not more than half a mile in front. He at the same time discovering them, put spurs to his horse, determined they should not overtake him. The cornet now put his horses to the top of their speed, and recollecting a short route through the woods, sent a party off that way, to intercept the road at a bridge below Bergen, while he with the remainder followed Champe. Being so closely pursued, Champe relinquished his intention of going to Paulus Hook, and sought refuge in some British galleys, that had for a long time occupied a station a few miles west of Bergen. On his entering the village he disguised his track by taking the beaten streets, and after passing through it, took the road leading to Elizabethtown. Meanwhile the cornet's party had reached the bridge, and found, with sore disappointment, the sergeant had slipped through their fingers. Returning up the road, they inquired whether a dragoon had been seen in the village, but could get no intelligence as to the road he had taken. The troops soon spread over the village, and in a short time again struck the trail. The chase was renewed with greater vigor, and Champe was soon discovered. He, apprehending the event, had prepared himself for it, as he now had come abreast the galleys. Leaving his horse, and lashing his valise to his shoulders, he threw himself into the river and called out to the galleys for aid. This was quickly given. The British fired on the cornet's party, and sent a boat to meet Champe, who was taken on board and conveyed to New York, with a letter from the captain relating the facts of the case. The cornet returned to camp in the afternoon, when the soldiers, seeing the sergeant's horse in his possession, exclaimed, " The scoundrel is killed and the honor of our corps vindicated."

When Champe arrived at New York, he delivered the letter from the captain of the galley to the commandant, and was soon sent to

---

private mark annexed to the fore shoe, and known to the troopers, pointed out the trail of the dragoons to each other, which was often very useful.

Lee's Memoirs.

Sir Henry Clinton. He detained him more than an hour, question-
ing him in reference to the state of the army since the desertion of
Arnold, the probable fate of Andre, and the popularity of Washington, all of which he answered warily. Placing two guineas in
his hand, he advised Champe to visit Arnold. On seeing him, the
traitor expressed great satisfaction, and pressed him to join a new
legion he was raising. After some delay, Champe enlisted, for the
purpose of securing the freedom of Arnold's house, which would
further the plans of taking him when the time should arrive.

He now turned his attention to the delivery of letters he had
brought, to the agents of Washington. On the following night he
delivered one, but it was not until five days after he saw the person
to whom the other was addressed, and who was to aid him in the
capture of Arnold. While these things were transpiring, Andre was
hung. Nothing now remained but to seize and deliver Arnol l safely
to Major Lee, who at an appointed time, was to be ready on the
Jersey shore to receive him. Champe, from his enlistment, had
every opportunity to notice the habits of Arnold. He discovered it
was his custom to visit the garden on his return home every night.
During this visit he was to be seized, gagged and carrie l into an
adjoining alley, where Champe's friends were to receive and bear
him to a boat in the North river.

On the night appointed, Major Lee left camp, with a body of
cavalry and three led horses, one for Arnold, one for Champe, and a
third for his friend ; never doubting the success of the adventure.
The party reached Hoboken about midnight, and concealed themselves in an adjoining wood. Lee, with three dragoons, went down
to the bank of the river. The night passed away, and no boat approached, when Lee returned to camp, much chagrined and disap-
pointed at the issue of the project.

Soon after, Lee received a letter from the friend of Champe, informing him that on the very night appointed for the execution of
the plot, Arnold had removed his quarters to another part of the
town, to superintend the embarkation of troops, and the corps to
which Champe belonged had already gone on board the transports.

Thus it happened that Sergeant Champe, instead of crossing the Hudson with his prisoner, was quietly placed on board a British transport, which he never departed from until the troops under Arnold landed in Virginia.

On the junction with Cornwallis, Champe deserted, passing into North Carolina and keeping within the friendly districts of that State, safely joined the American army, near the Congaree river. His old comrades were surprised to see *a deserter* so affectionately received by Major Lee, but after his story was told, cheer upon cheer went up for "the intrepid and gallant sergeant."

Lee's Memoirs.

[3] *A little hero.* This was Capt. Carnes, officer of the day, who communicated the fact of Champe's desertion to Major Lee.

Arnold.

1780

This " address to the vile traitor " was published in the Pennsylvania Packet, October 24th, 1780.

TO THE TRAITOR ARNOLD.

ARNOLD ! thy name, as heretofore,
Shall now be Benedict no more ;
Since, instigated by the devil,
Thy ways are turn'd from good to evil.

'Tis fit we brand thee with a name,
To suit thy infamy and shame ;
And since of treason thou'rt convicted,
Thy name should now be maledicted.

Unless by way of contradiction,
We style thee Britain's Benediction;
Such blessings she, with liberal hand,
Confers on this devoted land.

For instance, only let us mention,
Some proofs of her benign intention ;
The slaves she sends us o'er the deep,
The bribes to cut our throats in sleep.
To take our lives and scalps away,
The savage Indians keeps in pay,
And Tories worse, by half, than they.

Then in this class of Britain's heroes,
The Tories, savage Indians, Negroes,
Recorded, Arnold's name shall stand,
While Freedom's blessings crown our land.
And odious for the blackest crimes,
Arnold shall stink to latest times.

King's Mountain.

1780.

The success of the Americans at King's Mountain,[1] over the forces of Ferguson and Depuyster, has been the subject of numerous ballads. The one subjoined was written a short time after the action, and published on a small sheet, the following year.

BATTLE OF KING'S MOUNTAIN.[2]

'Twas on a pleasant mountain
  The Tory heathens lay;
With a doughty major at their head,
  One Ferguson they say.

Cornwallis had detach'd him,
  A thieving for to go,
And catch the Carolina men,
  Or bring the rebels low.

The scamp had rang'd the country
        In search of royal aid,
And with his owls, perchèd on high,
        He taught them all his trade.

But ah! that fatal morning,
        When Shelby brave drew near!
'Tis certainly a warning
        That ministers should hear.

And Campbell, and Cleveland,
        And Colonel Sevier,
Each with a band of gallant men,
        To Ferguson appear.

Just as the sun was setting
        Behind the western hills,
Just then our trusty rifles sent
        A dose of leaden pills.

Up, up the steep together
        Brave Williams led his troop,
And join'd by Winston, bold and true,
        Disturb'd the Tory coop.

The royal slaves, the royal owls,
    Flew high on every hand;
But soon they settled—gave a howl,
    And quarter'd to Cleveland.

I would not tell the number
    Of Tories slain that day,
But surely it is certain
    That none did run away.

For all that were a living,
    Were happy to give up;
So let us make thanksgiving,
    And pass the bright tin-cup.

To all the brave regiments,
    Let's toast 'em for their health,
And may our good country
    Have quietude and wealth.

[1] *King's Mountain* is situated near the Cherokee Ford, in the northern part of South Carolina. The battle ground is about one mile and a half south of the South Carolina line.

[2] *Battle of King's Mountain.* The following brilliant account of this action is taken from the oration of the Hon. J. T. Preston, delivered at the battle ground, on the 4th of October, 1855. The bat-

15

tle was fought on the 7th of October, 1780. "At twelve o'clock, the sky cleared," when the patriot army "found themselves within three miles of Ferguson's camp, on King's Mountain. They halted, under an order passed rapidly along the line—an order, perhaps, the most laconic and appropriate ever given under the like circumstances. It was in those words:

"'*Tie up overcoats, pick touch-holes, fresh prime, and be ready to fight.*'"

"The officers here determined to divide their force, and to surround the mountain. At this moment, an express from Ferguson to Cornwallis was arrested, his despatches opened, and read aloud at the head of the line. In them, he said, 'I hold a position on the King's Mountain that all the rebels out of hell cannot drive me from.' There was no shout or disorder when this was read; but a quiet grim smile passed along the line as they struck into a double gallop. In twenty minutes, they were in sight of the British camp. They drew up along the bank of that little brook; they dismounted and tied their horses to the limbs of ths trees, leaving them in charge of a small gui.rd. The order of attack was hurriedly made, but with a military skill and discretion that could not be excelled. There was not an error or mistake, or even a miscalculation of marching time from the outset to the end. Each column advanced rapidly along the indicated line, all the lines tending to a common centre, which was the British encampment at the summit of the ridge. There began a scattering fire, for eight or ten minutes, on the centre column of the Americans. The patriots moved steadily until Sevier's column, on the right, passed out of the valley in full sight of the enemy. The fire then began in earnest on both sides. The mountaineers proved their skill with most deadly effect, forcing Ferguson, at the very beginning, to resort to a direct charge. This charge was headed by a company of British regulars, and was worthy the high name and fame of that service. It was boldly and gallantly done, and forced the patriots to give back down the hill; but at that moment Cleaveland and Williams appeared on the left, and poured into the charging columns such an awful ire as to stop them before Sevier was routed. The British turned from charging on Sevier, and wheeling, made a terrible dash at Cleaveland and Williams on the left, and with like effect, driving them back down the ridge. Sevier, however, rallied instantly, and at the same time Shelby and Campbell appeared with the centre column, rising in front along the ridge. These two columns, the centre and left, then poured their fire on both flanks of the British, and stopped the charge against Cleaveland and Williams. Wheeling rapidly and receiving reinforcements from within the lines, the British then made a third charge directly against the centre column, and that irresistible British bayonet again told its story, and Campbell and Shelby were forced back, down nearly to the valley. But Cleaveland and Williams having rallied their columns, and Sevier's continuing to pour its fire in from the left, the British were forced to leave the pursuit of Campbell and Shelby, turned suddenly, and themselves retreated up the ridge. Shelby and Campbell, hearing this tremendous fire on both flanks, finding the British were retreating, supposed they were defeated, rallied instantly, and turned in pursuit of them with hurrahs of victory. The British turned immediately, and attempted a fourth charge. It, however, was then too late—the blood of the mountaineers was hot ; they met and repulsed that charge, and drove the British back within their lines. This enabled the three columns of the patriots to meet, and literally surround the army of Ferguson. Then came the fierce rage of the battle ; a circle of fire hemmed the wolf in his stronghold. The English soldiers proved their breeding in this hour of danger and despair. The regulars with their bayonets, and the Tories with their butcher-knives fastened to the muzzles of their guns, charged on this closing flame with the fierce energy of despair. In vain ! The mountain hunters, calmly but rapidly loading, and deliberately aiming, each at his mark, sent a death messenger in every bullet. At every discharge, they advanced a few steps, until there was one narrowing circle of flashing flame crackling around their devoted victims. At this moment, the British cavalry were ordered to mount. The order was heard by the Americans. It was the very thing for their rifles, giving a clear mark above the bushes; and as each man threw his leg over his horse, he fell dead on the other side. Ferguson, with a gallantry that seemed to rise with his desperate condition, rode from rank to rank, and from post to post, encouraging, cheering, and driving his men. At length, he found his army pressed, and actually huddled together near the summit of the mountain, and falling·as fast as the Americans could load and shoot. He determined on one more charge, and, taking his position at the head of his cavalry, and with a voice that was heard loud above the roar of battle, summoned his men to 'crush the damned rebels into the earth.' There was a pause for a moment, and one round of the Americans was stopped. Instead of the roar of their rifles, there was heard only the click of the lock—it was the serpent's low warning of coming death. The pause was but for a moment, when Ferguson and Dupoistre, horse and foot, burst like an avalanche down the mountain's side. Before they came within sixty paces of the American line, every rifle was loaded and under deadly aim. Ferguson was in front, and fell at the first discharge, with seven mortal wounds. The patriots rushed forward to meet the shock as Dupoistre's regulars, with set bayonets and sabres in rest, came crushing down upon them. Not Agincourt nor Cressy, with all their chivalry, ever felt a shock more fearful than that; but had the heavens rained British bayonets, it would not have stopped these patriots. The destinies of America, perhaps of mankind, depended on their muscle. Like martyrs, they went to the death—like lions they rushed to the carnage. Officer and soldier, with blood-shot eyes and parched tongues, bounded upon the huddling enemy until their fierce glare and hot breath could be seen and felt by the craven Tory and his bull-dog master; and at the moment they were crouching together for the last spring, a wild, terror-stricken shriek rose above the battle—a yell for quarter. A white flag was run up, arms thrown down, and God's champions shouted, 'Victory! Liberty!' That shout echoed from the mountain to the sea, and far along the shore to where the majestic Washington sat almost weeping over the sad horrors of the South. His great heart leaped with prophetic joy as this beam of hope came borne on the triumphant voice of his beloved and trusted men of 'West Augusta;' for the men who sent that shout were the very men of whom Washington said he would 'trust to them to maintain American liberty after all else had failed.' He knew the mountain was the birthplace, but never the grave, of liberty. One hour sufficed for this crowning scene in the swelling drama of our Revolutionary struggle, acted by rude men from beyond 'unknown mountains.' Not one of the enemy escaped. The force of Ferguson amounted to something over eleven hundred men, and of these two hundred and forty were killed, and two hundred wounded—a strange proportion, telling the fatal story of that long small bore rifle. Over seven hundred were taken prisoners, with all their arms, ammunition, and equipments. It was a total defeat, and a capture of nearly a quarter of Cornwallis's army."

New Year's Day.

1781.

This production was written in America, and published in a music sheet, entitled "New Year's Day, 1781, to the tune "*Get you gone, raw head and bloody bones*." It also appeared in the anti-ministerial English and American newspapers of the time.

NEW YEAR'S DAY.

Oh! old England, old England;
    And oh! the New Year's day;
Such a new year as this
    A blind man would gladly see.
        How we go up, up, up, &c.

Now we are at a dead stop,
    And so we sink deeper and deeper ,
Little Georgey's as sound as a top,
    And his Primy's an excellent sleeper.

Oh ! the navy, the navy,
    Of Britain the safety and boast;
Lord Twitcher has kept it so safely,
    Our foes on the seas rule the roast.

Here's an inferior fleet,
    With an admiral wrapt up in flannel ;
By which we're insulted abroad,
    And with which we sneak into the channel.

But oh ! how we hurried and scurried,
    Our cowardly enemies scorning ;
There we run away over night,
    And there we waited till morning.

Parliaments squabble and gabble,
    Ministers wonder and stare ;
Armies march backwards and forwards,
    Americans stand as they were.

But oh ! how bloody and stout,
    Struts the commander-in-chief;
He's as sharp as a snipe at the snout,
    And lacks nothing but wisdom and beef.

This lord bids him go up,
That lord makes him run down,
T'other drives him first backwards and forwards,
And a fourth makes him skip and turn round.

With such mighty armies and fleets,
With commanders and ministers true ;
We bully all kingdoms and states,
Tho' to beat one we cannot tell how.
But so we go up, up, up, &c.

As for our credit and wealth,
The pride and the strength of John Bull;
The nation's as poor as myself,
Tho' Lord North swears his budget's quite full.
So we go up, up, up, &c.

Oh! for a gibbet and block,
Oh! for a hatchet and cleaver;
How well would a home-hit stroke,
Prove a just and a kind reliever.
Then would old England go up,
Instead of going down, down-a;
We're tired of backwards and forwards,
'Tis time that things were turn'd round-a.

Then would we lop 'em and crop 'em,
    Bring traitors at once to a level;
The junta should lead up the dance,
    And the others the way to the devil.
            Then would old England go up, &c.

At court we make snuffers and buttons,
    Great folks must have something to do;
Bully Bagshot cures drunkards and gluttons,
    The king gallops from Windsor to Kew.
            See him tit up a tit up, &c.

Oh! religion, religion,
    I mean to be seriously grave,
Archbishops and bishops raise papists,
    The protestant cause for to save.
            So we go up, up, up, &c.

See Murray and Wedderburne both,
    O'er our lives and our fortunes preside;
And its lucky for England, in troth,
    No such lawyers are bred south of Tweed.
            So we go up, up, up, &c.

15*

So we're abolish'd, demolish'd,
 Yet no man stands up for his right;
But, my friends, while the kingdom's on fire,
 The Scots make their way by the light.
 Then help old England up,
 And knock all her enemies down,
 Let us join as all Englishmen ought,
 'Tis time that things were turn'd round.

A Song.

1781.

THE SOLDIER AT HOME.

From noise of camps once more I come,
    To snatch from care a short repose ;
All hail thou tranquil much lov'd home,
    That war nor dread misfortune knows.

Thus, far remov'd from hostile bands,
    May'st thou heart-pleasing home remain ;
Curs'd be the murderous foreign hands
    That dare with blood thy bosom stain.

Oh haste, ye generous few I love,
  Again in social converse join;
With me the sweets of friendship prove,
  And to the winds your cares resign.

But oh ! to recollect how soon
  The period comes that bids me hence;
A sadd'ning momentary gloom
  Steals half my joys, and clouds my sense.

But why indulge that care-mix'd thought ?
  The happy day may yet arrive,
When tyranny shall fall to nought,
  And liberty alone survive.

Then with my friends in jocund mood,
  I'll tell what dangers have been mine;
And how Americans have stood
  At Germantown and Brandywine.

Here we'll remember martial Gates,
  He taught the proud Burgoyne to yield;
Who frowning at his adverse fates,
  Surrender'd on the well fought field.

Then each gay friend shall swell the tale,
　With hardy deeds of bold emprise;
Again he sees our arms prevail,
　And long-lost ardors now arise.

Here Howe, says he, (and marks the track,)
　The British troops did proudly form;
And here with adverse lines compact,
　Brave Washington did swell the storm.

'Twas here I was, and points the spot,
　(As he had tracèd on the ground,)
What bursts of thunder, showers of shot,
　Yet there great Washington was found.

At Monmouth's plains, where Lee retreated,
　Great Washington did then push on;
Sir Harry's chosen troops defeated,
　Then laugh'd his tyranny to scorn.

These happy days are yet to come,
　Then why repine at such a fate;
Bear well the woe that is your doom,
　And joy can never come too late.

Descent on Middlesex.

1781.

On the evening of the twenty-first of July, seventeen hundred
and eighty-one, a party of Refugees embarked at Lloyd's Neck, on
Long Island, and landed on the Connecticut shore the same night.
The party concealed themselves in a wood, about five miles from the
place where they landed, and near the meeting-house of the town
of Middlesex. Here they lay until two o'clock in the afternoon of
the next day, " when the good people of Middlesex were assembled,
and devoutly praying for their great and good ally, the King of
France, the brave party surrounded their sanctuary, and took from
thence fifty notorious rebels ; their reverend teacher at their head.
Their horses, forty in number, saddled and at hand, were taken care
of at the same time. The whole were moved in the most expedi-
tious manner to the shore, during which the rebels, in the vicinity of
Middlesex, collected and harassed the soldiers in their return, notwithstanding which, every rebel and every horse captured were
safely conducted on board the armed vessels, which returned to

Lloyd's that night." [1]   The writer of this ballad, schoolmaster St. John, of Norwalk, was one of the persons taken by this party.   He composed it a short time after he returned to his home from the Provost at New York.

DESCENT ON MIDDLESEX.

JULY the twenty-second day,
The precise hour I will not say,
In seventeen hundred and eighty-one,
A horrid action was begun.

While to the Lord they sing and pray,
The Tories who in ambush lay ;
Beset the house with brazen face,
At Middlesex, it was the place.

A guard was plac'd the house before,
Likewise behind and at each door ;
Then void of shame, those men of sin,
The sacred temple enter'd in.

The reverend Mather [2] closed his book,
How did the congregation look !
Those demons plunder'd all they could,
Either in silver or in gold.

The silver buckles which we use,
Both at the knees and on the shoes,
These caitiffs took them in their rage,
Had no respect for sex or age.

As they were searching all around,
They several silver watches found ;
While they who're plac'd as guards without,
Like raging devils rang'd about.

Run forty horses to the shore,
Not many either less or more ;
With bridles, saddles, pillions on,
In a few minutes all was done.

The men from hence they took away,
Upon that awful sacred day,
Was forty-eight, besides two more
They chanc'd to find upon the shore.

On board the shipping they were sent,
Their money gone, and spirits spent,
And greatly fearing their sad end,
This wicked seizure did portend.

They hoisted sail, the Sound they cross'd,
And near Lloyd's Neck they anchor'd first;
'Twas here the Tories felt 'twas wrong,
To bring so many men along.

Then every man must tell his name,
A list they took, and kept the same;
When twenty-four of fifty men
Were order'd to go home again.

The twenty-six who staid behind,
Most cruelly they were confin'd;
On board the brig were order'd quick,
And then confin'd beneath the deck.

A dismal hole with filth besmear'd,
But 'twas no more than what we fear'd;
Sad the confinement, dark the night,
But then the devil thought 'twas right.

But to return whence I left off,
They at our misery made a scoff;
Like raving madmen tore about,
Swearing they'd take our vitals out.

They said no quarter they would give,
Nor let a cursèd rebel live;
But would their joints in pieces cut,
Then round the deck like turkeys strut.

July, the fourth and twentieth day,
We all marched off to Oyster Bay;
To increase our pains and make it worse,
They iron'd just six pair of us.

But as they wanted just one pair
An iron stirrup lying there,
Was taken and on anvil laid,
On which they with a hammer paid.

And as they beat it inch by inch,
It bruis d their wrists, at which they flinch;
Those wretched caitiffs standing by,
Would laugh to hear the sufferers cry.

Although to call them not by name,
From Fairfield county many came;
And were delighted with the rout,
To see the rebels kick'd about.

At night we travell'd in the rain,
All begg'd for shelter, but in vain ;
Though almost naked to the skin,
A dismal pickle we were in.

Then to the half-way house we came,
The " Half-way House " 'tis called by name,
And there we found a soul's relief ;
We almost miss'd our dreadful grief.

The people gen'rously behav'd,
Made a good fire, some brandy gave,
Of which we greatly stood in need,
As we were wet and cold indeed.

But ere the house we did attain,
We trembled so with cold and rain,
Our irons jingled—well they might—
We shiver'd so that stormy night.

In half an hour or thereabout,
The orders were, " Come, all turn out !
Ye rebel prisoners, shabby crew,
To loiter thus will never do."

'Twas now about the break of day,
When all were forc'd to march away;
With what they order'd we complied,
Though cold, nor yet one quarter dried.

We made a halt one half mile short
Of what is term'd Brucklyn's fort;
Where all were hurried through the street:
Some overtook us, some we met.

We now traversing the parade,
The awful figure which we made,
Caus'd laughter, mirth, and merriment,
And some would curse us as we went.

Their grandest fort was now hard by us,
They shew'd us that to terrify us;
They shew'd us all their bulwarks there,
To let be known how strong they were.

Just then the Tory drums did sound,
And pipes rang out a warlike round;
Supposing we must thence conclude,
That Britain ne'er could be subdu'd.

Up to the guard-house we were led,
Where each receiv'd a crumb of bread ;
Not quite one mouthful, I believe,
For every man we did receive.

In boats, the ferry soon we pass'd,
And at New York arriv'd at last ;
As through the streets we pass'd along,
Ten thousand curses round us rang.

But some would laugh, and some would sneer,
And some would grin, and others leer ;
A mixèd mob, a medley crew,
I guess as e'er the devil knew.

To the Provost we then were haul'd,
Though we of war were prisoners call'd ;
Our irons now were order'd off,
And we were left to sneeze and cough.

But oh ! what company we found,
With great surprise we look'd around :
I must conclude that in that place,
We found the worst of Adam's race.

Thieves, murd'rers, and pickpockets too,
And every thing that's bad they'd do;
One of our men found to his cost,
Three pounds, York money, he had lost.

They pick'd his pocket quite before
We had been there one single hour;
And while he lookèd o'er and o'er,
The vagrants from him stole some more.

We soon found out, but thought it strange,
We never were to be exchang'd
By a cartel, but for some men
Whom they desir'd to have again.

A pack with whom they well agree,
Who're call'd the loyal company,
Or " Loyalists Associated,"
As by themselves incorporated.

Our food was call'd two-thirds in weight
Of what a soldier has to eat;
We had no blankets in our need,
Till a kind friend did intercede.

Said he, " The prisoners suffer so,
'Tis quite unkind and cruel too;
I'm sure it makes my heart to bleed,
So great their hardship and their need."

And well to us was the event,
Fine blankets soon to us were sent;
Small the allowance, very small,
But better far than none at all.

An oaken plank, it was our bed,
An oaken pillow for the head,
And room as scanty as our meals,
For we lay crowded head and heels.

In seven days or thereabout,
One Jonas Weed was taken out,
And to his friends he was resign'd,
But many still were kept behind.

Soon after this some were parol'd,
Too tedious wholly to be told;
And some from bondage were unstrung,
Whose awful sufferings can't be sung.

The dread smallpox to some they gave,
Nor tried at all their lives to save,
But rather sought their desolation,
As they denied 'em 'noculation.

To the smallpox there did succeed,
A putrid fever, bad indeed;
As they before were weak and spent,
Soon from the stage of life they went.

For wood we greatly stood in need,
For which we earnestly did plead;
But one tenth part of what we wanted
Of wood, to us was never granted.

The boiling kettles which we had,
Were wanting covers, good or bad;
The worst of rum that could be bought,
For a great price, to us was brought.

For bread and milk, and sugar, too,
We had to pay four times their due;
While cash and clothing which were sent,
Those wretched creatures did prevent.

Some time it was in dark November
But just the day I can't remember;
Full forty of us were confin'd
In a small room both damp and blind,

Because there had been two or three,
Who were not of our company,
Who did attempt the other day,
The Tories said, to get away.

In eighteen days we were exchang'd,
And through the town allowed to range;
Of twenty-five that were taken,
But just nineteen reach'd home again.

Four days before December's gone,
In seventeen hundred eighty-one,
I hail'd the place where months before,
The Tories took me from the shore.

[1] Letter from Colonel Upham, Commandant at Lloyd's Neck, to Governor Franklin of New Jersey.

[2] *The reverend Mather.* Moses Mather, D. D., was the pastor of the church. He was taken prisoner in 1779 by a gang of loyalists, and carried to New York. At this time, the members of his con-

gregation were taken out of the church, tied two and two, with Dr.
Mather at their head. Cunningham, the keeper of the Provost at
New York, took every opportunity to insult Dr. Mather during his
imprisonment, and seemed to have great satisfaction in informing
him from day to day, " that he would soon be executed—very probably, on the morrow."

The Dance.

1781.

This song, to the tune of Yankee Doodle, commemorating the campaign of Cornwallis in America, appeared soon after his surrender. The author is unknown.

THE DANCE.[1]

CORNWALLIS led a country dance,
　　The like was never seen, sir,
Much retrograde and much advance,
　　And all with General Greene, sir.

They rambled up and rambled down,
　　Join'd hands, then off they run, sir,
Our General Greene to Charlestown,
　　The earl to Wilmington, sir.

Greene, in the South, then danc'd **a set,**
   And got a mighty name, **sir,**
Cornwallis jigg'd with young **Fayette,**
   But suffer'd in his fame, sir.

Then down he figur'd to the shore,
   Most like a lordly dancer,
And on his courtly honor swore,
   He would no more advance, sir.

Quoth he, my guards are weary grown
   With footing country dances,
They never at St. James's shone,
   At capers, kicks or prances.

Though men so gallant ne'er were seen,
   While sauntering on parade, sir,
Or wriggling o'er the park's smooth **green,**
   Or at a masquerade, sir.

Yet are red heels and long-lac'd **skirts,**
   For stumps and briars meet, sir ?
Or stand they chance with **hunting-shirts,**
   Or hardy veteran feet, sir ?

Now hous'd in York he challeng'd all,
    At minuet or all 'amande,
And lessons for a courtly ball,
    His guards by day and night conn'd.

This challenge known, full soon there came,
    A set who had the bon ton,
De Grasse and Rochambeau, whose fame
    Fut brillant pour un long tems.

And Washington, Columbia's son,
    Whom easy nature taught, sir,
That grace which can't by pains be won,
    Or Plutus' gold be bought, sir.

Now hand in hand they circle round,
    This ever-dancing peer, sir;
Their gentle movements, soon confound
    The earl, as they draw near, sir.

His music soon forgets to play—
    His feet can no more move, sir,
And all his bands now curse the day,
    They jiggèd to our shore, sir.

Now Tories all, what can ye say ?
   Come—is not this a griper,
That while your hopes are danc'd away,
   'Tis you must pay the piper.

[1] *The Dance.* The troops under Cornwallis had spread desolation and ruin throughout the country over which they passed on their march from the South. Their numbers enabled them to go wherever they pleased, with comparatively little danger, and their great hatred to the Yankees, often led them far from the line of march, to the wanton destruction of property and life. The defeat and capture of such an army produced the strongest emotions in the breasts of the Colonists, and their villages, in their houses and their streets, resounded with the tokens of social triumph, exultation and joy.

Cornwallis Burgoyned.

1781.

Several songs were composed to commemorate the surrender of the royal army at Yorktown. The one subjoined was published a short time after the event, adapted to the air "Maggie Lauder," which was at that time a great favorite in both armies.

CORNWALLIS BURGOYNED.

WHEN British troops first landed here,
　　With Howe commander o'er them,
They thought they'd make us quake for fear,
　　And carry all before them;
With thirty thousand men or more,
　　And she without assistance,
America must needs give o'er,
　　And make no more resistance.

But Washington, her glorious son,
    Of British hosts the terror,
Soon, by repeated overthrows,
    Convinc'd them of their error ;
Let Princeton, and let Trenton tell,
    What gallant deeds he's done, sir,
And Monmouth's plains where hundreds fell,
    And thousands more have run, sir.

Cornwallis, too,¹ when he approach'd
    Virginia's old dominion,
Thought he would soon her conqu'ror be;
    And so was North's opinion.
From State to State with rapid stride,
    His troops had march'd before, sir,
Till quite elate with martial pride,
    He thought all dangers o'er, sir.

But our allies, to his surprise,
    The Chesapeake had enter'd ;
And now too late, he curs'd his fate,
    And wish'd he ne'er had ventur'd,

For Washington no sooner knew
   The visit he had paid her,
Than to his parent State he flew,
   To crush the bold invader.

When he sat down before the town,
   His Lordship soon surrender'd ;[2]
His martial pride he laid aside,
   And cas'd the British standard;[3]
Gods! how this stroke will North provoke,
   And all his thoughts confuse, sir!
And how the Peers will hang their ears,
   When first they hear the news, sir.

Be peace, the glorious end of war,
   By this event effected ;[4]
And be the name of Washington,
   To latest times respected;
Then let us toast America,
   And France in union with her,
And may Great Britain rue the day
   Her hostile bands came hither.

[1] *Cornwallis, too.* Cornwallis was a distinguished warrior, intrepid and confident, and a zealous champion of his tyrannical master.

16*

" Had all the *rebels* in the States but *one neck*, his Lordship would **glory** in nothing more than an opportunity of *severing* the *jugular vein.*"

[2] *His Lordship soon surrender'd.* The siege of Yorktown continued thirteen days, when Cornwallis requested a suspension of hostilities, during which time he made a desperate attempt to escape. On the morning of the day appointed for the laying down of arms, the American and French troops were drawn up on either side of the road, in a line of more than a mile in length. At about two o'clock in the afternoon the captive army advanced through the line, led by General O'Harra, who Cornwallis had appointed as substitute, he pretending sickness. O'Harra, advancing to the head of the lines, approached General Washington, and taking off his hat, apologized for the non-appearance of Earl Cornwallis. With his usual dignity and politeness, his Excellency pointed to General Lincoln for directions; by whom the British army was conducted to the place where it was intended they should lay down their arms. It was here, when they came to the last act of the drama, that the spirit and pride of the British soldier was put to the severest test, and their mortification and disappointment could not be concealed. The subjoined epigram appeared a short time after the surrender :

> The Earl Cornwallis, who ought to be civil,
> Grows gouty and sore, and sends us the devil;
> For who is the leader on us he doth parry,
> But Brigadier-general and tory 'OHarra.

[3] *And cas'd the British standard.* The terms of capitulation were similar to those granted to General Lincoln, at Charleston, the preceding year. The troops marched out with shouldered arms, colors cased, and drums beating a British march. It was very gratifying to General Lincoln to have assigned him the duty of giving laws to the haughty army, which a few months before had obliged him to surrender, and of reflecting that the terms which were imposed on him, were adopted as a basis in the present instance.

[4] *By this event effected.* This event was looked upon as the closing **scene** of the Continental war in America.

The South Carolina.

1782.

On Thursday night, the nineteenth of December, at 10 o'clock, off the Delaware, the British ships, Quebec, Diomede and Astrea, carrying ninety-eight guns, fell in with the American ship South Carolina, of forty guns, having under convoy a ship, brigantine and a schooner, bound out from Philadelphia. The South Carolina was chased eighteen hours, when she fired a stern chase at the Diomede, which was returned by one of the latter's bow-guns. After a running fight of more than two hours, the American colors were struck to the British.

THE LETTER.[1]

My dear brother Ned,
We are knock'd on the head;
No more let America boast;
We may all go to bed,
And that's enough said,
For the South Carolina we've lost.[2]

The pride of our eyes,
I swear is a prize,
You never will see her again,
Unless thro' surprise,
You are brought where she lies,
A prisoner from the false main.

Oh Lord ! what a sight—
I was struck with affright,
When the Diomede's shot round us fell,
I feared that in spite,
They'd have slain us outright,
And sent us directly to h——l.

The Quebec did fire,
Or I'm a curs'd liar,
And the Astrea came up apace ;
We could not retire,
From the confounded fire,
They all were so eager in chase.

The Diomede's shot
Was damnation hot,
She was several times in a blaze ;

It was not my lot,
To go then to pot,
But I veow, I was struck with amaze.

And Ned, may I die,
Or be pok'd in a sty,
If ever I venture again
Where bullets do fly,
And the wounded do cry
Tormented with anguish and pain.

The Hope, I can tell, [3]
And the brig Constance fell,
I swear, and I veow, in our sight;
The first I can say,
Was taken by day,
But the latter was taken at night.

I die to relate
What has been our fate, [4]
How sadly our navies are shrunk;
The pride of our State,
Begins to abate,
For the branches are lopp'd from the trunk.

The Congress must bend,
We shall fall in the end,
For the curs'd British sarpents are tough ;
But, I think as you find,
I have enough penn'd
Of such cursèd, such vexatious stuff.

Yet how vexing to find,
We are left all behind,
That by sad disappointment we're cross'd ;
Ah, fortune unkind !
Thou afflicted'st my mind,
When the South Carolina we lost.

Our enemy vile,
Cunning Digby does smile,
Is pleasèd at our mischance ;
He useth each wile,
Our fleets to beguile,
And to check our commerce with France.

No more as a friend,
Our ships to defend,
Of South Carolina we boast ;

As a foe in the end

She will us attend,

For the South Carolina we've lost

[1] *The Letter.* This ballad appeared in the loyal papers, as a letter "from a dejected Jonathan, a prisoner taken in the South Carolina, to his brother Ned at Philadelphia."

[2] *For the South Carolina we've lost.* She was bound on a cruise off Charleston, South Carolina, and was taken the day after she sailed. She was built in Holland in 1778. Her keel was about one hundred and sixty feet long, and as strong as a castle. Captain Joiner commanded her in this action. The Americans' loss in killed and wounded was fourteen, and that of the British very slight. "Fifty German and eight British soldiers of General Burgoyne's army, who had been taken out of jail at Philadelphia, and compelled on board the Carolina, rather than submit to be sold by the rebels, were on this occasion happily released from a service so obnoxious to their principles." *Loyal prints.*

[3] *The Hope, I can tell.* The ship Hope and the brig Constance were the vessels taken in company with the South Carolina. The little schooner escaped and reached Charleston in safety.

[4] *What has been our fate.* A few days after the action, the South Carolina arrived at New York and anchored in the East River. The newspapers of that city, in announcing her arrival, say, that "she was to call at Charleston and there receive Commodore Gillon on board, but being *imperfectly coppered* by the rebels at Philadelphia, it was judged expedient to alter her destination, and bring her round to New York to complete her sheathing, only *thirteen feet* of which had been performed."

Thanksgiving Hymn.

1783.

The following composition was originally intended to be sung on the Thanksgiving Day, appointed in consequence of the peace between the United States and Great Britain in 1783, but was not published until some years after that event. It is a fine specimen of the " patriotic hymns and psalms " of that period.

THANKSGIVING HYMN.

THE Lord above, in tender love,
 Hath sav'd us from our foes;
Through Washington the thing is done,
 The war is at a close.

America has won the day,
 Through Washington, our chief;
Come let's rejoice with heart and voice,
 And bid adieu to grief.

Now we have peace, and may increase
　　In number, wealth, and arts ;
If every one, like Washington,
　　Will strive to do their parts.

Then let's agree, since we are free,
　　All needless things to shun ;
And lay aside all pomp and pride,
　　Like our great Washington.

Use industry, and frugal be,
　　Like Washington the brave ;
So shall we see, 'twill easy be,
　　Our country for to save,

From present wars and future foes,
　　And all that we may fear ;
While Washington, the great brave one,
　　Shall as our chief appear.

Industry and frugality,
　　Will all our taxes pay ;
In virtuous ways, we'll spend our days,
　　And for our rulers pray.[1]

The Thirteen States, united sets,
　In Congress simply grand ;
The Lord himself preserve their health,
　That they may rule the land,

Whilst every State, without its mate,
　Doth rule itself by laws,
Will sovereign be, and always free ;
　To grieve there is no cause.

But all should try, both low and high,
　Our freedom to maintain ;
Pray God to bless our grand Congress,
　And cease from every sin.

Then sure am I, true liberty
　Of every sort will thrive ;
With one accord we'll praise the **Lord**,
　All glory to Him give.

To whom all praise is due always,
　For He is all in all ;
George Washington, that noble one,
　On His great name doth call.

Our Congress too, before they do,
   Acknowledge Him supreme;
Come let us all before Him fall,
   And glorify His name.

[1] *And for our rulers pray.* From among the hymns written on
the return of peace, we select the following unique specimen, from
a composition by Oliver Arnold, the author of the parody on the
" Banks of the Dee."

> " Come, let us shout! and praise the Lord!
>   What hath he left undone?
> Let's shout for him, and sing to him,
>   He gave us Washington!
> Let's shout to him, and pray to him,
>   And pray for Washington! "

𝔄 𝔉ragment

1 7 8 3 .

This ballad, by Robert Burns, is familiar to every one. Chambers, in his Life and Works of the Poet, says, the production "is curious, as an example of that brief direct narration in which the rustic mind usually gives its version of the most complicated political and historical transactions."

A FRAGMENT.[1]

WHEN Guildford good our pilot stood,
 And did our helm thraw, man,
Ae night, at tea, began a plea,
 Within America, man ;
Then up they gat the maskin'-pat,
 And in the sea did jaw, man ;
And did nae less, in full Congress,
 Than quite refuse our law, man.

Then through the lakes Montgomery takes,
    I wat he was na slaw, man ;
Down Lowrie's burn he took a turn,
    And Carleton did ca', man ;
But yet, what-reck, he, at Quebec,
    Montgomery-like did fa', man,
Wi' sword in hand, before his band,
    Amang his en'mies a', man.

Poor Tammy Gage, within a cage,
    Was kept at Boston ha', man ;
Till Willie Howe took o'er the knowe
    For Philadelphia, man ;
Wi' sword and gun he thought a sin
    Guid Christian blood to draw, man :
But at New York, wi' knife and fork,
    Sir-loin he hackèd sma', man.

Burgoyne gaed up, like spur and whip,
    Till Fraser brave did fa', man ;
Then lost his way, ae misty day,
    In Saratoga shaw, man.

Cornwallis fought as lang's he dought,
 And did the buckskins claw, man ;
But Clinton's glaive frae rust to save,
 He hung it to the wa', man.

Then Montague, and Guildford too,
 Began to fear a fa', man :
And Sackville dour, wha stood the stoure,
 The German Chief to thraw, man ;
For Paddy Burke, like ony Turk,
 Nae mercy had at a', man ;
And Charlie Fox threw by the box,
 And lows'd his tinkler jaw, man.

Then Rockingham took up the game,
 Till death did on him ca', man ;
When Shelburne meek held up his cheek,
 Conform to gospel law, man ;
Saint Stephen's boys, wi' jarring noise,
 They did his measures thraw, man,
For North and Fox united stocks,
 And bore him to the wa', man.

Then clubs and hearts were Charlie's cartes,
 He swept the stakes awa', man,
Till the diamond's ace, of Indian's race,
 Led him a sair faux pas, man;
The Saxon lads, wi' loud placads,
 On Chatham's boy did ca', man;
And Scotland drew her pipe and blew,
 ' Up, Willie, waur them a', man! '

Behind the throne then Grenville's gone,
 A secret word or twa, man;
While slee Dundas aroused the class,
 Be-north the Roman wa', man;
And Chatham's wraith, in heavenly graith,
 (Inspirèd Bardies saw, man)
Wi' kindling eyes cried, ' Willie, rise !
 Would I hae fear'd them a', man ? '

But, word and blow, North, Fox and Co.,
 Gowff'd Willie like a ba', man,
Till Southron raise, and coost their clase
 Behind him in a raw, man;

And Caledon threw by the drone,
  And did her whittle draw, man ;
And swoor fu' rude, through dirt and blood,
  To make it guid in law, man.

---

[1] *A Fragment.*   This ballad was adapted to the tune Killiecrankie, a Gælic air, composed, it is said, by the pipe-major of the old Highland regiment, known to the world by the title of " The XLII. Regiment of Royal Highlanders," or as Cook, the celebrated actor, used to style it, " *the brave forty-twa.*"

Burns, at the time he wrote these verses, says Chambers, was in "in a raw and unenlightened state as a politician."   In a letter to the Hon. Henry Erskine, in reference to this ballad, Burns says, " I showed the enclosed political ballad to my Lord Glencairn, to have his opinion whether I should publish it ; as I suspect my political tenets, such as they are, may be rather heretical in the opinion of some of my best friends.   I have a few first principles in religion and politics, which, I believe, I would not easily part with ; but for all the etiquette of, by whom, in what manner, &c., I would not have a dissocial word about it with any one of God's creatures, particularly an honored patron or a respected friend.   His lordship seems to think the piece may appear in print, but desired me to send you a copy for your suffrage."

A Sonnet.

1783.

The author of these verses, Colonel David Humphreys,[1] "the soldier-poet of the revolution," was born at Derby, Connecticut, in the year 1752, and graduated at Yale College in 1771.

ON DISBANDING THE ARMY.[2]

Ye brave Columbian bands! a long farewell!
Well have ye fought for freedom—nobly done
Your martial task—the meed immortal won—
And Time's last records shall your triumphs tell.

Once friendship made their cup of suff'rings sweet—
The dregs how bitter, now those bands must part!
Ah! never, never more on earth to meet;
Distill'd from gall that inundates the heart,
What tears from heroes eyes are seen to start!

17

Ye, too, farewell, who fell in fields of gore,

And chang'd tempestuous toil for rest serene ;

Soon shall we join you on the peaceful shore,

(Though gulfs irremeable roll between),

Thither by death-tides borne, as ye full soon have been.

[1] *David Humphreys.* Soon after Humphreys graduated, he went to reside with Colonel Phillips, of Phillips Manor, New York. He joined the Continental army, and in 1778 became one of General Putnam's aids, with the rank of Major. In 1780 he was promoted to be aide-de-camp to Washington, with the rank of Colonel. He continued in the family of the Commander-in-Chief during the war, and after the resignation of the General, accompanied him to Mount Vernon. For his valor at Yorktown, Congress honored him with a sword. On the appointment of Mr. Jefferson, as ambassador to France, Col. Humphreys was nominated as Secretary to the Legation, and for the first time left his native country, in 1784. In 1786, he was a member of the Connecticut Legislature, and about that time he, Barlow, and Hopkins wrote the *Anarchiad.* In 1790, he was appointed Minister to Portugal, and afterwards Minister Plenipotentiary to Spain. His literary attainments were considerable. Besides several poems, he wrote various political pamphlets, and completed a life of General Putnam, which is included in a volume of his works.

[2] *On disbanding the army.* It will be difficult for any person who was not present with the troops at the conclusion of the war, to form an adequate idea of the affecting circumstances which attended the disbanding of the army. *Note by the author of the sonnet.*

INDEX.

17*